Budgeting in Higher Education

J. Kent Caruthers and Melvin Orwig

AAHE-ERIC/Higher Education
Research Report No. 3, 1979

Prepared by the
ERIC ® Clearinghouse
on Higher Education
The George Washington University
Washington, D.C. 20036

Published by
the American Association
for Higher Education
One Dupont Circle, Suite 780
Washington, D.C. 20036

This publication was prepared pursuant to a contract with the National Institute of Education, U.S. Department of Health, Education and Welfare. Contractors undertaking such projects under government sponsorship are encouraged to express freely their judgment in professional and technical matters. Prior to publication, the manuscript was submitted to the American Association for Higher Education for critical review and determination of professional competence. This publication has met such standards. Points of view or opinions do not, however, necessarily represent official views or opinions of either the American Association for Higher Education or the National Institute of Education.

Acknowledgments

When Jonathan Fife invited us to prepare this AAHE-ERIC/Higher Education Research Report on budgeting and budget planning, we were grateful for the opportunity (and aware of the attendant obligation) to collect and organize our thoughts on this topic. We regard it as important to everyone with an interest, selfish or otherwise, in higher education. After some months of effort, however, the initial sense of pleasure had shaded toward distress. The limit on manuscript pages, the magnitude of our subject, and the diversity of postsecondary education in America, compounded to make our elected task seem too ambitious. We wanted the monograph to be academically sound, to have pragmatic value for the budgeting practitioner, and to be relevant to the concerns of administrators in all types of postsecondary-education institutions. But there simply was not space to do all that.

So we sought remedies, the first of which was our publisher's kind permission to submit a somewhat longer manuscript than originally contemplated. And we determined to narrow our scope, to concentrate on budgeting in collegiate institutions, rather than trying to embrace the concerns of the full, diverse set of schools that constitute postsecondary education. Even so, we found it necessary, within the scope of higher education, to focus most of our remarks on budget planning in state-supported institutions.

Nonetheless, we hope that this manuscript will interest those concerned with independent colleges and various other kinds of institutions found in postsecondary education. We concede that these readers may find that various examples of fine points in the budgeting process we offer are not altogether applicable to their own situations. We have tried to provide a reasonable, comprehensive, balanced view of budgeting — a format with the busy college executive in mind.

If our attempt to cover such a broad topic in a limited compass produced its frustrations, they were more than compensated by the attendant refreshment of our own thinking and the opportunity to take advantage of the perspectives of our colleagues at the National Center for Higher Education Management Systems. Ben Lawrence, Richard Allen, Frank Armijo, William Johnston, Wayne Kirschling, Sid Micek, and Jim Topping all shared their expertise to illuminate various aspects of the monograph. We are grateful to each of them.

We benefited greatly also from the comments of seven outside reviewers, who represent a remarkable amalgam of academic and pragmatic understanding of finance and higher education. They are Brenda Norman Albright, Associate Director for Fiscal Affairs and Data Systems for the Tennessee Higher Education Commission; Professor Lyman A. Glenny of the University of California, formerly Executive Director of the Illinois Board of Higher Education; Dr. Hans Jenny, Vice President for Finance and Business at the College of Wooster; Professor Larry Leslie of the University of Arizona, Office of Research and Study in Higher Education; Dr. Anthony Morgan, Assistant to the Vice President and Assistant Professor of Higher Education at the University of Utah; Gail Norris, Executive Coordinator of the Washington Council of Postsecondary Education and former Director of Planning and Budget Officer at the Pennsylvania State University; and Professor Augustus Turnbull, former Staff Director of the Florida House of Representatives Committee on Education and now Chairman of Florida State University's Department of Public Administration. Each of these reviewers submitted many helpful comments and the monograph is clearly more valuable to its readers because of their efforts.

Finally, we wish to express our appreciation to several members of the NCHEMS staff who helped prepare the manuscript. In particular, we are indebted to Karon Kelly who provided library support services, to Paula Dressler and Helen Barron who typed the early versions of the manuscript and helped us maintain an accurate bibliography, and to Barbara Epp and Linda Priddy who typed the final manuscript.

Lest the reader suspect that we are conniving to share the blame for any inadequacies in the monograph with 19 others, we hereby declare ourselves fully responsible for all omissions or errors.

J. Kent Caruthers and Melvin D. Orwig

Foreword

A "budget" is defined by *Webster's New Collegiate Dictionary* as: a statement of the financial position of an *administration* for a definite period of time based on estimates of expenditures during the period and proposals for financing them; a plan for the coordination of *resources* and *expenditures* (emphasis added).

For higher education there are two areas in developing a budget that make this process considerably different from that of a commercial business. First and foremost, the goals of business are usually very straightforward — to make a profit — and are set by management. In higher education the goals are not singular but are a balancing of teaching, research, and service activities. The emphasis and resources directed toward each area are not determined solely by management but are the result of general understanding between faculty and administration.

The second difference is income. For business, income is determined by the price placed on its goods or services and the quantity sold. The price is set to exceed the expenses needed to produce the goods or services; the quantity sold is determined by the production capacity and sales force of the business. For higher education the price of the product is set at far below cost, thus necessitating that the institution look for revenue from other sources to break even. For example, in 1975-76, for all of higher education, only 20.6 percent of income came from student tuition and fees. The remaining income came from the federal government (16.3 percent); state government (4.1 percent); private gifts, grants, and contracts (4.1 percent); endowments (1.7 percent); sales and services (19.4 percent); and other sources (2.2 percent). Thus, institutions of higher education are dependent on many sources of income, many that are not directly related to the student or to the research capacity of an institution.

Because of institutions' inability to clearly set goals and the multiple sources of revenue, the budgeting process has not been well understood by most of the institutions' members. This was not a great concern while institutions were growing and funds were plentiful. But in the face of declining enrollment, decreasing government support, and a static faculty, it is becoming increasingly important to have a wide understanding of the budgeting process to influence this process.

Kent Caruthers, Senior Staff Associate, and Melvin D. Orwig, Associate Director, at the National Center for Higher Education Management Systems (NCHEMS) have developed a Research Report that brings together the major actors, procedures, and systems involved in the budgeting process. Their review and analysis of this process points out how budgets are created, the importance they play in setting policy, and how the various levels of the institution can have input into this process.

Jonathan D. Fife, Director
ERIC ® Clearinghouse on Higher Education

Contents

Overview

Administrators in postsecondary education often regard budgeting as primarily a financial exercise — necessary, but dull and tedious. Budgeting is, however, one of the most dynamic functions of management, because it affects all management functions. As Aaron Wildavsky observed:

> . . . one is likely to think of budgeting as an arid subject, the province of stodgy clerks and dull statisticians. Nothing could be more mistaken. Human nature is never more evident than when men are struggling to gain a larger share of funds or to apportion what they have among myriad claimants (1974, p. xxiii).

The essential purposes of budgeting are to distribute resources, translate plans into actions, and foster accountability. In its most basic conception, the budget is an instrument that enables the allocation of resources from one organizational unit to another, whether it be from a department to a faculty member, from a college to a department, from the university to a college, or from a funder to the university. In allocating these resources, however, explicit choices are made among alternative ways in which they might be used.

Typically, the request budget (which indicates what resources are sought and for what purposes) is larger than the expenditure budget (which specifies the uses of the resources actually provided). In formulating the request budget, choices are made at each level, from faculty member to academic chief executive, regarding the possible activities that might be carried out at the institution during the budget period. Similarly, the translation of the request budget into the spending budget involves making choices among the proposed set of activities. Most choices made in the annual request-allocation cycle focus on how to spend the proposed budget increment. Since the increment usually is small by contrast with the existing budget base, one iteration of the annual cycle seldom has dramatic impact on institutional direction. Significant programmatic change and budget reallocation normally result from special planning studies. Nonetheless, much attention and energy are focused on the annual budget cycle. Various techniques and approaches — the executive budget; planning, programming, and budgeting systems (PPBS); zero-base budgeting; formula budgeting; performance-based budgeting; as well as various

1

modifications or combinations of these — represent efforts to improve the processes by which request budgets are developed and decisions reached to transform them into spending budgets.

The budget also is the formal mechanism through which plans become undertakings. Not all agree, however, that the planning and budgeting functions should be completely integrated. Schmidtlein and Glenny (1977), Pyhrr (1973), and Schick (1966) argue that planning and budgeting inherently conflict. They note, for example, that planning tends to go forward without the specific resource or time constraints that apply in the budget process (Schmidtlein and Glenny 1977, p. 240). On the other hand, Hitch (1967) contends that separation of planning and budgeting functions was a major source of difficulty in the Department of Defense, providing the primary rationale for the introduction of PPBS into that agency. Whether or not planning and budgeting are carried out by the same staff or are totally integrated, organizational plans eventually must be translated into some formal budget request if they are to become operational activities. This essential relationship between planning and budgeting cannot be ignored.

The third general purpose of the budget, at all organizational levels, is to serve as an instrument for achieving both internal and external accountability. Internally, budgets provide a mechanism for expenditure and management control of operational activities. Externally, the budget helps to communicate to constituencies the activities that will be supported by allocations and the expected results. To the extent that the results are or are not achieved, the credibility of the organization is enhanced or reduced.

And so the making of a budget should not be treated as a routine exercise. The budget — its development, communication, and execution — lies at the heart of the management process and affects, directly or indirectly, most management decisions. In this monograph, we undertake to identify the forces and factors shaping current approaches to budgeting in postsecondary education and to indicate likely developments in coming years.

Major Issues and Implications

We begin this six-part monograph with a brief review of a long-standing debate concerning whether budgeting is largely a technical or a political exercise. Two equally plausible arguments command our attention. There is much to be said for developing and improving technical approaches to budgeting. The budget must be reduced to quantitative form, and the use of technical analyses in all forms of decisionmaking is well established. Just as clearly, however, budgeting requires choices in a political environment. The importance of people, of their values and convictions, cannot be estimated by a standard process or reduced to a number. Although the debate sometimes takes on either-or dimensions, we conclude that good budgeting practice must draw from both of these perspectives and be tailored to the situation at hand. The challenge to the budget planner is to understand the proper application of each consideration, human and numerical.

The next section considers several major issues that emerge in almost any discussion of budgeting. We analyze the roles of various participants in the budgeting process and the form of their participation, with emphasis on a key participation theme — centralization of authority in the budgetary process. The problem of equity — allocating similar resources for similar needs — is also explained. Finally, we discuss the roles of various types of information, particularly that pertaining to the costs and outcomes of the educational experience in budgetary decisionmaking, and the burdens of information reporting. In some form or other, these themes have appeared in the literature at least since Trevor Arnett's seminal work on higher-education finance in 1922. We conclude that these issues do not lend themselves to general solutions, and thus reason that they will always be sources of concern in budget development.

Like most administrative activity, current budgetary practice results from an evolutionary process. The third section of the monograph traces the heritage of current budget-planning approaches in postsecondary education. We consider the approaches to budgeting in private industry and trace the development of budgeting practice in the public sector during this century. We then describe the particular problems associated with budgeting in postsecondary education and discuss the influence of the business and public-administration approaches. The third section closes with a discussion of why the demands for greater rationality in budgeting are caused by emerging issues such as the projected enrollment decline, the movement by many institutions to serve new clientele or enter new markets or both, the ever-increasing demands for accountability, and the emergence of collective bargaining.

In the fourth section, we describe in detail five budget-planning approaches: incremental budgeting, formula budgeting, program budgeting, zero-base budgeting, and performance budgeting. All these approaches are used in postsecondary education today. We observe a definite trend toward the so-called more rational budgeting approaches in our ever-changing environment, and find further support for our conclusion that more budget innovation in the rationalist stream is probable during the coming decade.

The fifth section presents an analysis of budgetary roles and responsibilities existing at different organizational levels and how they vary as the function of particular phases of the resource-request-allocation cycle. We consider budget-request strategies and budget-review techniques, finding that the considerable uncertainty that deans and department heads must cope with until the allocation is known leads to considerable tension and frustration.

Recommendations for Further Inquiry

If, as we concluded, budgeting in postsecondary education is likely to undergo significant change in the coming decade, what might be done that would encourage positive results? We conclude that there are a number of needed research and development activities surrounding the major issues that we identify in the monograph.

Further research is needed in at least the following three areas:

• *Understanding the fixed and variable nature of resource consumption in higher education* — a better knowledge of cost behavior is essential for successful development of new approaches to state-level funding, improved pricing decisions, cost recovery, and identification of the short-term financial impacts of retrenchment decisions.

• *Understanding the organizational and decisionmaking processes in budgeting* — more work is needed in evaluating the comparative effectiveness of decisions that are made at various levels of the budget process and in assessing the role of technical analysis in support of the political nature of budgeting.

• *Understanding the impact of entering new markets* — budgeters need to be able to provide considerably more information about the long-term fiscal and pragmatic consequences of changing their mission to serve new markets.

We also see the need for four general categories of applied research and development:

• *Integrating academic planning and budgeting activities* — there will be a strong tendency for planners to ignore the pragmatic implications of budget reductions when faced with retrenchment, but such shortsightedness will lead to even more complex problems in later years.

4

• *Adapting budgeting techniques to the unique needs of colleges and universities* — since most budget reform occurs outside the confines of higher education, developmental activities will be required to modify emerging budgeting techniques to make them more valuable for institutions of higher education.

• *Measuring financial implications of collective bargaining* — collective bargaining is increasingly becoming the way of life for both academic and nonacademic staffs. Given the tendency for unions never to give back any advantage gained, budget planners need an improved ability to evaluate the long-term financial implications of each collective bargaining demand.

• *Improved enrollment forecasting* — the major advances achieved in enrollment forecasting a decade ago are best suited for anticipating growth and capital construction needs. New methods are required that are more accurate and that can determine probable enrollments at more discrete levels. Beyond that, enrollment projection models should be developed than can reflect the consequences of management efforts to increase enrollment (for example, initiation of student marketing programs), rather than have enrollment projections based exclusively on demographic trends.

Because of space limitations, emphasis in the monograph is placed on the budgetary process in public institutions and state-level postsecondary-education agencies. Relatively little attention is devoted to federal concerns, practices in private institutions, revenue forecasting, or budgeting for restricted funds. The monograph does not attempt to explain how to carry out budgeting. Our purpose is to provide a general background about the issues, techniques, and developments in postsecondary budgeting and to acquaint the reader with the extensive literature that is available for further investigation.

Budgeting Perspectives

Budgeting is most frequently considered from a technical perspective. A budget is variously described as a financial plan (Heckert and Willson 1955) and a planning and control system (Jones and Trentin 1966). Heiser (1959), however, distinguishes between the passive nature of a budget and the active process of budgeting. He defines a *budget* as an overall blueprint or a comprehensive plan of operations and actions, expressed in financial terms. He views *budgeting,* on the other hand, as the process of preparing a budget, a function that is used for planning and coordination as well as for maintaining management control of the organization. Thus the two principal aspects of budgeting are budget planning and budget control.

Pyhrr (1973) attempts to distinguish between planning and budgeting, describing planning as the process that identifies desired outputs, and budgeting as the process that identifies required inputs. Yet his description of zero-base budgeting links the planning and budgeting functions, thereby introducing a new concept, that of a budgeting system. Jones and Trentin succinctly capture most of the technical aspects of a budget, budgeting, and a budgeting system.

> A budget can be regarded as primarily a plan or goal or objective, and we know of no better definition of budgeting than to say it is primarily a *planning* and *control system*. Each word in that definition is important for a full understanding of budgeting's proper role. The planning and control aspects relate to the fundamentals of the management process. . . . To regard budgeting as a system is most important, because this implies a continuing process throughout the year — the key to good budgeting in any business operation (1966, p. 14).

Yet even this technical definition, comprehensive though it is, does not embrace the full substance of budgeting and its impacts. Wildavsky points out that budgeting cannot be disassociated from its participants.

> Budgeting deals with the purposes of men. How can they be moved to cooperate? How can their conflicts be resolved? . . . Serving diverse purposes, a budget can be many things: a political act, a plan of work, a prediction, a source of enlightenment, a means of obfuscation, a mechanism of control, an escape from restrictions, a means to action, a brake on progress, even a prayer that the powers that be will deal gently with the best aspirations of fallible men (1974, p. xxiii).

Human Elements

As the importance of the interaction between people and budgets becomes more clearly understood, increasing attention is paid by social psychologists and organizational theorists to budgeting (Glenny 1976a, pp. 12-32). Similarly, the valuative dimensions of budgeting, which are manifestations of human values, social forces, and political processes, are emerging in the literature to claim equality with the scientific dimensions associated with techniques, systems, and quantitative analysis.

In part, this is explained by the complexity that derives from the diversity characterizing the constituencies of postsecondary education and from the many perspectives represented by the participants in the budgetary process. Students, faculty, institutional administrators, state executives and legislators, and federal executives and legislators are all directly affected by and involved in the process. Each of these groups is, to a greater or lesser degree, a consumer of services provided by postsecondary education. As such, each group has an interest in the prices for services, which are determined in the budgetary process, and in the programmatic decisions made during the development of a budget or forced by budget constraints (Morgan 1975).

When resources are limited, a decision to increase resources for instruction can result in decreased resources for research, less emphasis on public service, a reduction in student health services, higher student fees or tuition, and so forth. Thus such a decision can coincide with the interests of some students and faculty and contravene the interests of others. (Recognizing the pervasive influence of the budget, the American Association of University Professors has adopted a formal policy statement on the role of the faculty in budgeting matters (AAUP 1976).) Similarly, the same decision might satisfy legislators interested in improved instruction, yet conflict with state and federal programs designed to improve financial access to postsecondary education. Balancing these diverse interests is an important role of the budgetary process, and the impact of the process clearly transcends the purely technical dimensions of any particular budgeting system.

Technical Analysis

Few would argue that budgeting is simply a technical exercise carried out in a routinized system. Nonetheless, there is considerable intellectual disagreement about the role of quantitative analysis and systems in budgeting (Glenny et al. 1975; Meisinger 1975; Morgan

7

1978; Schick 1971; Schmidtlein and Glenny 1977; Schultze 1968; and Wildavsky 1974). The roots of this debate can be traced to a central problem in welfare economics regarding the optimal distribution of resources between the government and the private sector (Musgrave and Peacock 1958). Though there are many technical and philosophical facets to this debate, inevitably welfare economics is premised and dependent on a political mechanism that enables social values to be identified and expressed in public policy and to be served through public programs (Dahl and Lindblom 1953).

In recent years, attention has focused on different approaches to budgeting and on organizational interactions, both external and internal, associated with budgeting systems. The development of the planning, programming, and budgeting system (PPBS) did more to heighten this debate than any other single development — witness Nelson's bibliography on program budgeting, which has 1,054 entries (1970).

PPBS is typical of budgeting systems in that it was introduced to (1) achieve better coordination between the planning and budgeting functions, (2) enable consideration of future consequences of budget decisions, (3) improve understanding of how proposed expenditures influence programs, and (4) make the budget an instrument for achieving a greater congruence between an organization's goals and its programs. Hitch glowingly summarized the results of the implementation of PPBS in the Defense Department:

> Thus, we have provided for the Secretary of Defense and his principal military and civilian advisors a system which brings together at one place and at one time all of the relevant information that they need to make sound decisions on the forward program and to control the execution of that program. . . . Now, for the first time, the largest business in the world has a comprehensive Defense Department-wide plan that extends more than one year into the future (1967, p. 39).

Assessments like these led to the eventual implementation of PPBS in all federal agencies and the increasing use of program-oriented budgeting in state governments.

Political Rationality

Not everyone is as optimistic about technical approaches to budgeting, however. Wildavsky, for example, contends that more recent analytical approaches to budgeting have tended to emphasize the achievement of economically efficient programmatic alternatives at the expense of politically sound and acceptable policies. In developing the case for political rationality, Wildavsky quotes the philosopher Paul Diesing:

> . . . the political problem is always basic and prior to all the others.
> . . . This means that any suggested course of action must be evaluated
> first by its effects on the political structure. A course of action which
> corrects economic or social deficiencies but increases political difficulties
> must be rejected, while an action which contributes to political improvement
> is desirable even if it is not entirely sound from an economic or
> social standpoint (1974, p. 191).

The need for political rationality derives from the "political costs," as Wildavsky terms them, incurred in the development and establishment of public policy. Wildavsky views them as exchange costs,

> incurred by a political leader when he needs the support of other people
> to get a policy adopted. He has to pay for this assistance by using up
> resources in the form of favors (patronage, logrolling) or coercive moves
> (threats or acts to veto or remove from office). By supporting a policy
> and influencing others to do the same, a politician antagonizes some
> people and may suffer their retaliation. If these hostility costs mount,
> they may turn into reelection costs — actions that decrease his chances (or
> those of his friends) of being elected or reelected to office. Election costs,
> in turn, may become policy costs through inability to command the
> necessary formal powers to accomplish the desired policy objectives. . . .
> In a political situation, then, the need for support assumes central importance.
> Not simply the economic, but the *political* costs and benefits
> turn out to be crucial (1974, p. 192).

In constructing a model of state postsecondary-education budgeting, Schmidtlein and Glenny proposed three criteria by which to measure the effectiveness of the budget process: technical efficiency, allocative efficiency, and rationality. "Technical efficiency," they explain, "denotes the degree to which an organization produces a set of outputs of specified quality and quantity using the least cost set of inputs and processes" (1977, p. 27). Allocative efficiency is concerned with the relative preferences of collective and individual members of society regarding the distribution of the costs and benefits of budgeted activities. Using a somewhat unusual concept of rationality that is probably allied to the Dahl and Lindblom contention that bargaining is a politico-economic necessity (1953), Schmidtlein and Glenny put forward the rationality criterion as a means of focusing on the bargaining process. The rationality criterion recognizes that many questions do not "open up" for straightforward technical or allocative analysis and, as a consequence, require a budgetary process that permits discussion and negotiation.

The rationality criterion is particularly important when outputs are obscure or controversial. In this circumstance,

> a process is designed that permits affected parties to evaluate the consequences of decisions and to bargain for favorable outcomes. Outcomes result from this multilateral bargaining process and not from comprehensive analysis and decisions by a central decisionmaker (1977, p. 30).

Wildavsky is clearly more concerned about allocative efficiency and rationality than he is about technical efficiency. He argues strongly against the particular form of budgeting represented by PPBS and is concerned about the drive to increase technical efficiency in budgeting practices. But the main thrust of his discourse is to promote budgeting processes that allow for political negotiation. Though for the most part cast negatively, his argument can be viewed as a positive statement for more attention to rationality, the third criterion identified by Schmidtlein and Glenny. On the role of analysis in budgeting, Wildavsky is more ambiguous:

> Studies based on efficiency criteria are much needed and increasingly useful. My quarrel is not with them as such, at all. I have been concerned that a single value, however important, could triumph over other values without explicit consideration being given these others. I would feel much better if political rationality were being pursued with the same vigor and capability as is economic efficiency. In that case I would have fewer qualms about extending efficiency studies into the decision-making apparatus (1974, p. 194).

Analysis and Decisionmaking

Schultze is a more open advocate of the need for technical analysis in budgeting. He nonetheless recognizes the importance of politics in budgeting. Through the political process, he observes, human values are interjected into decisions: "In a democracy, the political tools of decisionmaking — bargaining, advocacy, negotiation, and compromise — are the means by which workable agreements are made amid conflicts about values and interests" (1968, p. vii). But analysis is really important. "Analysis," Schultze maintains, "can help focus debate upon matters about which judgments are necessary. It can suggest superior alternatives, eliminating or at least minimizing the number of inferior solutions. Thus by sharpening the debate, systematic analysis can enormously improve it" (1968, p. 75). In other words, analysis can refine the options from which alternatives are chosen and in that way help to improve the quality of decisions.

Summing up his explication of the role of quantitative analysis in policy development and budgeting, Schultze observes:

> The most frustrating aspect of public life is not the inability to convince others of the merits of a cherished project or policy. Rather it is the endless hours spent on policy discussions in which relevant issues have not been separated from the irrelevant, in which ascertainable facts and relationships have not been investigated but are the subject of heated debate in which consideration of alternatives is impossible because only one proposal has been developed, and, above all, discussions in which nobility of aim is presumed to determine effectiveness of program.
>
> There are enough real value conflicts, institutional rigidities, and scarcities of information in the way of effective government action. Let us not add a massive additional obstacle by assuming that complex values can be effectively translated into necessarily complex programs by nothing more than spirited debate.
>
> It may, indeed, be necessary to guard against the naivete of the systems analyst who ignores *political* constraints and believes that efficiency alone produces virtue. But it is equally necessary to guard against the naivete of the decisionmaker who ignores *resource* constraints and believes that virtue alone produces efficiency (1968, pp. 75-76).

Clearly, both politics and quantitative analysis have important roles in budgeting. Political negotiation provides a mechanism through which social and human values can be reflected in budgetary decisions. Quantitative analysis, on the other hand, helps to refine options, explore the consequences of alternatives, and thereby helps to sharpen the debate. As Glenny observes:

> Despite disagreement and lack of theory, budget professionals are moving slowly and pragmatically toward a more systematic approach to budgeting. They attempt to apply common procedures and practices . . . and to gain objectivity in budget decisionmaking through data and information systems, use of analytic simulations and decision models, and new forms of budgets, generally program types of budgets. While we encourage these efforts . . . we agree with Dror who states that "to be frank, neither the facts nor the methods needed to set down a complete. basic guide for constructing optimal policymaking systems are yet available." (1976a, p. 8).

The reason for Dror's caution is exemplified in the work of Pfeffer and Salancik. Relying on the work of organizational scholars[1] for

---

[1] Analysis of organizations from the perspective of decisionmaking has been carried out for several years and a rich literature surrounds it. But as Pondy has noted, ". . . sociologists . . . have tended not to focus on the resource allocation problem" (1970, p. 271).

Both Glenny (1976a) and Schmidtlein and Glenny (1977) offer an excellent discussion of the interrelationships of organization and budget theory. Beyond that are the works of Baldridge (1971), Cyert and March (1963), Downs (1967). March and Simon (1958), and Thompson (1967), all concerned with organizational theory and decisionmaking processes.

11

the construction of their analytical paradigm, they found that the amount of resources provided to departments was directly related to the power (political influence) held by that department in the organization. "The more powerful the department, the less the allocated resources are a function of departmental workload and student demand for course offerings" (1974, p. 135). Thus to understand budgeting in postsecondary education, one must be aware of both the political and analytical dimension of budgeting.

As Dahl and Lindblom point out, "not all of everyone's goals can be satisfied in economic life. Economizing, therefore, requires a process for determining whose goals shall have priority and to what extent" (1953, p. 129). These priorities are determined and decisions made through a combination of political negotiation and technical analysis. Though the literature is replete with arguments for and against both, their separation is artificial and misleading.

Technical analysis in budgeting is not a substitute for politics. It will not, nor should it, seek to eliminate politics from planning and budgeting. It is through the political process that values and intuitive judgments are incorporated into decisions. Analysis can help, however, to focus discussions, identify alternatives, and assess the possible future consequences of a particular course of action. Provided they are not viewed and used as ends in themselves, we regard technical approaches to budgeting as necessary adjuncts to decisionmaking in an increasingly complex environment.

Major Issues in Postsecondary
Education Budgeting

Given the diverse and far-reaching purposes served by budgeting, it should not be surprising that many issues, many points of contention, surround budgeting in postsecondary education. Though the issues are interrelated in their effects, we have, for purposes of discussion, organized them into five categories: participation, centralization of authority, equity, information burdens, and cost, outcomes, and performance information.

In *The Uses of the University*, Kerr (1963) coined *multiversity* to connote the complexity of the modern American university. It is an enterprise conducted by individuals exhibiting more differences in interests than they share in common and serving diverse and often conflicting purposes. Balderston has noted that universities are "(mostly, but not entirely) focused on the young and paid for by the old . . . they are supposed to endure forever, and they make their budgets one uncertain year at a time" (1963, p. 1). He adds:

> the general goals of a university are shrouded in vagueness. By common consent, there are several goals, but there is not consensus among those concerned with universities about the relative importance of the goals, the interdependencies among them, or ways of measuring attainment of them (1974, p. 9).

The vagueness and lack of consensus are logical consequences of the manner in which goals are articulated. Balderston again:

> goals are worked out by numerous accommodations in the organization rather than, as may appear, being adopted and announced from on high. . . . In short, we deal with the operation and design of a *managerial process* and not the question of coaching a single executive to do the right thing. . . . There are many contributors to the managerial process, differently situated in the university — some with administrative titles and others without (1975, pp. 4-5).

The same might be said of the budgeting process in collegial institutions. Not all agree that this diffuseness regarding institutional goals is either desirable or necessary. Neff, for example, argues that

> . . . university goals should be centrally derived. Goals — broad statements of the institutional purpose — should be an expression of the total institutional perspective. The total perspective is always more than the sum of the desires of subgroups within the institutions (1971, p. 124).

Participation

Nonetheless, Balderston has captured the current state of participatory decisionmaking in universities and other senior educational institutions. Faculty, students, and administrators are all effected by, and therefore desire to participate in, the development of the institutional budget. Externally, the interests of the alumni, the community, and, if it is a publicly funded institution, state agencies and legislators along with federal administrators must also be considered in the development of a budget. As Balderston points out,

> the university has become a mixture of institution, enterprise, and agency. This is partly because it has assembled a large and confusing range of activities and operations, but partly also because the major parties at interest want to view it in different ways: the faculty and students, as an institution; the trustees and some administrators, as an enterprise; and the governmental sponsors, as an agency. Conflicts of purpose, law, motivation, and style flow from these different views (1974, p. 2).

Participation in budgeting is further complicated by the unique roles of faculty and students. On the one hand, faculty, as teachers and researchers, participate in the organization in traditional labor roles. On the other hand, as the designers of programs, the developers of disciplines, the directors of research projects, and the maintainers of academic standards, faculty perform management roles. Their claim to participation in the development of the budget is therefore on the basis of two roles of equal import (AAUP 1976).

Similarly, students function in a dual capacity. As consumers, they are interested in the choices made in the budgetary process. Through their individual decisions to enroll or not enroll in particular courses or programs, they can impact budgetary choices. They also affect budget decisions through their participation in campus governance. On the other hand, students can be regarded as products of the institution. In this capacity, however, they have less claim to participation in the institutional budgetary process.

Balancing the diverse interests of these participants in postsecondary education and satisfying their claims for equal participation is a major challenge in the development of budgets. The problem is further exacerbated, as Shick observes, by the fact that

> Budgeting is characterized by two opposing tendencies. . . . It is at once a highly fragmented and a highly interdependent process. Fragmentation comes from the dispersion of political power, the tradition of building budget requests from the bottom-up, and the heterogeneous roles and interests of budget officers, operating officials, elected executives, and legislators. Interdependence is an inherent characteristic of all budgeting, de-

riving from the scarcity of resources and the necessity to secure the co-operation of many parties in the making of expenditure policy. Budgeting can be interpreted as an effort to impose some coordination in the face of the centrifical pressures of agencies and interests (1971, p. 185).

Centralization of Authority

As budgeting approaches have been developed that try to counter the fragmentation inherent in postsecondary education and to achieve greater commonality of purpose and thrust through the budgeting process, concerns about centralization have emerged. The relationship of budgeting to centralization of authority within organizations and among organizations and agencies is treated extensively in the literature. This should not be surprising; in many ways whether authority is seen to be properly located or exercised depends on the eye of the beholder.

Faculty members, for example, who feel that the department chairperson did not consult them sufficiently in the preparation of the departmental budget are likely to think that the budgeting process was too centralized. The department chairperson, on the other hand, might feel that the dean of the college developed the college budget without appropriate consultation at the departmental level — and so on up the line. It is an unavoidable fact of budgeting that there are seldom enough resources to do everything. Some requests will be supported and some will not. When budget decisions are made, either implicitly or explicitly, authority is exercised. Whether those decisions are made at the appropriate level and whether the authority is exercised by the right actors are points of major contention.

In considering the requests of an individual institution, should a state agency, the legislature, or the institution decide whether a particular program should be initiated or whether funds should be expanded on specific activities? Should the legislature provide a lump sum of resources and allow the institution, through its own processes, to determine how they will be used? The same questions can be asked of university-wide administrations in relation to the operation of individual colleges and of college deans with regard to the operation of specific instructional programs, research activities, or departmental activities. Frequently, procedures and controls established by central authorities for the budget process later act as incentives, intended or unintended, in developing or executing the budget. Examples include the requirement to expend all resources by the end of the year, controls on specific line items such as travel or hiring procedures, or the kind of student credits that are eligible for funding.

15

The Center for Research and Development in Higher Education at the University of California in Berkeley conducted one of the most comprehensive studies of state budgeting for postsecondary education. The studies focused on state budgeting and financing of higher education and resulted in several important and useful reports.[2] A common theme in each of these reports, developed most extensively in Glenny (1976) and Schmidtlein and Glenny (1977), is the growing staff dominance in state budgetmaking, the increasing redundancy of effort among state agencies in reviewing institutional budgets, a corresponding increase in the burdens imposed on institutions, and the erosion of institutional decisionmaking authority. Glenny points out:

> As monitoring staffs increase so does their control over myriad items and policy matters embedded in the budgets. Ziegler, deputy commissioner for higher education in Pennsylvania, pleads the institution's case: "In the last analysis, therefore, those who establish the funding levels and set priorities within the budget determine how the institution will function. To the extent that those decisions are now made by legislative committees and their staffs, and by the governor's budget director and staff, control over the institution's destiny has passed out of the hands of the institution's officers and faculty. I think that this has been a clear tendency during the past decade (1976, p. 72).

Similarly, the Carnegie Foundation for the Advancement of Teaching notes:

> . . . the overall tendency toward centralization of authority over higher education — from the campus to the multicampus system, and from governing boards to state mechanisms. We regret this because: It reduces the influence of students and of faculty members and of campus administrators and of members of campus governing boards. . . . It also reduces their sense of responsibility. . . . This centralization seems to have had no measurable direct impacts on policies or on practices. . . . The governance processes are worse. They are more costly, more cumbersome, more time-consuming, more frustrating, and place more power in the hands of those who are the furthest removed and who know the least (1976, pp. 11-12) .

A common objective of recently developed budgetary procedures is to achieve greater consistency in the information used in formulating budget requests within institutions and among institutions within systems. While consistency is necessary for systematic analysis of budget requests, Cheit (1973) suggests that it can also lead to the

---

[2]Glenny et al. (1975) ; Bowen, Ruyle, and Glenny (1976); Ruyle and Glenny (1976) ; Schmidtlein and Glenny (1977); Purves and Glenny (1976); Glenny (1976a); Meisinger (1976); and Bowen and Glenny (1976) .

elimination of diversity and increased centralized direction of higher education.

Thus it can be observed that the budgetary process indeed may lead to the centralization of authority in postsecondary education. In the abstract, however, this is not necessarily undesirable, according to McNamara: "Vital decision-making, *particularly in policy matters, must remain at the top*. This is partly, though not completely, what the top is for" (1968, pp. 109-10).

Neff's view is that "the ideal situation is achieved when decentralization of activity and initiative is combined with a commonly oriented attentiveness to institution-wide purposes. Centralization and decentralization far from being mutually exclusive, are, in the right mix, both complementary and necessary" (1971, p. 125). Nonetheless, the issue of centralization is likely to remain a point of contention in budgeting as long as choices must be made and decisions rendered. Though most participants in a budgetary process would subscribe to a principle that would enhance the operational flexibility of those responsible for carrying out activities, this inclination is counterbalanced by the desire to contain this flexibility within some limits of acceptable performance. Thus the two ends of the continuum — the desirability of flexibility and the necessity for accountability — interact at various levels of the postsecondary-education budgetary process in such a way that issues related to centralization of authority are not likely to diminish.

Equity

A frequent objective of budgeting in postsecondary education is to achieve equity in the funding that is provided. As used in these discussions, the concept of equity implies that similar resources will be provided for similar individuals, similar programs within an institution, or similar institutions within a state system. One procedure used, particularly at the state level, to accomplish this purpose — formula budgeting — attempts to relate the allocation of resources to standard, consistent measures of an activity. Halstead points out that "formulas have achieved *acceptability* among users who appreciate equitable treatment based on sound rationale" (1974, p. 663).

The effective use of formulas is complicated by the unique characteristics of individuals, programs, and institutions. While it may be desirable to provide similar funding for similar activities, the critical variable in this equation is the identification of similarity or

17

sameness. New programs are likely to require more resources than well-established programs. An institution that is growing in enrollment is likely to find itself in a different situation than a similar institution that has recently experienced a serious enrollment decline. Therefore, Holmer and Broomfield maintain that

> one of the fundamental properties of a well-designed allocation model is its ability to reflect those institutional differences in missions, roles, and physical plants which require special funding consideration [but that] institutions should be provided with "equal pay for equal work" regardless of their overall role and mission in the State (1976, p. 3).

Formulas do offer many advantages, and they can routinize difficult decisions and help achieve a more equitable approach to the allocation of resources (Meisinger 1976). But they also can run counter to another important objective of budgeting, which is to treat each request on its own merits. Equality of funding is sensible only if a large degree of commonality exists among the purposes of individuals, programs, and institutions. To the extent that diversity is valued in postsecondary education, however, different budget procedures and processes are required. Thus it is argued that formulas that attempt to achieve equality of funding also tend to encourage standardization and discourage diversity. They may also create budgeting incentives that cause institutions to act counter to their mission. Thus, an important principle of formula budgeting is that the formulas should accommodate unique circumstances and provide differential treatment where warranted by institutionally accepted policy objectives.

Other concepts of equity exist, however. In elementary and secondary education, equity refers not only to equal funding but to equalization of property-tax expectations among school districts (Odden 1978). Other budgeting approaches also deal with equity, but in different ways. PPBS, for example, would have all programs evaluated by the same technique — cost-benefit analysis. And a common approach to incremental budgeting is to provide the same increment, on a percentage basis, to all departments.

In these circumstances, the concept of equity in postsecondary-education budgeting is complex at best and frequently misunderstood. Many maintain that attempts to achieve equity run counter to traditions of diversity in higher education. But the Holmer-Broomfield concept of equity suggests that it is achieved only when institutional differences are recognized in the funding formula. Viewed from this perspective, objectives of equity and diversity are less in conflict than might appear on the surface.

Information Burdens

One of the costs of budgeting is the technical information used in the particular budgeting approach. Information costs are determined by the kinds of data systems needed to provide the required information as well as the personnel costs of generating, formatting, checking, transmitting, and analyzing the information. Different budgeting approaches require different kinds and amounts of information about different subject matter and at varying levels of detail.

Therefore, a range of issues related to the information used in budgeting is considered in the literature. At the most basic level are questions about the quantity of information required to support different approaches. At a more technical level are important questions about the measurement and use of such concepts as costs, outcomes (benefits), and performance. These concerns are not a recent phenomenon, as evidenced by the 1935 report of the National Committee on Standard Reports for Institutions of Higher Education:

> In the past, there has been no uniformity whatsoever in the demands made by different governmental bodies or agencies or even by different divisions of the same government. This situation *has placed an excessive burden on many institutions* and has made accurate statistics of higher education a practical impossibility. It should be possible to establish a standard report and classification which will set forth facts needed for all types of financial reports and at the same time will supply essential information needed for internal administration (1935, p. 4; emphasis added).

Several efforts have been undertaken over the years to achieve better consistency in the information used in postsecondary education. In recent years, the National Center for Higher Education Management Systems has developed information procedures that are widely used by institutions and state agencies, and the National Center for Education Statistics publishes several manuals to support the annual Higher Education General Information Survey. Because of these developmental efforts, it has been possible to improve the consistency of budgeting information. This has not, however, always decreased information burdens in budgeting.

Another factor that tends to increase the data burdens of budgeting occurs when changes are made to the budgeting system or approach. Because it is important, for comparative and analytic purposes, to use standardized data definitions and collection procedures, a change in budgeting procedures can impact data procedures embedded in institutional information systems. The consequence may be extensive reprogramming costs or increased personnel costs if the information must be assembled by hand. Schmidtlein and Glenny point out that

> A major change in the format of budgets disrupts the whole system. Usually new kinds of data must be collected and aggregated in different ways. Users must adjust to the loss of old data and learn to use the new data (1977, p. 196).

Thus the nature of the budgeting approach, the need for standard data definitions and procedures, and changes in budget formats can all lead to increased information costs. Nonetheless, the Carnegie Foundation favors "basing budget actions on the best information, the best analyses, and the best judgment of highly qualified persons" (1976, p. 12) — even though the Foundation has not observed this happening very often. In any case, Schmidtlein and Glenny offer this wise caution:

> Budget processes must be designed to provide consistent data on areas of policy concern in a format that permits easy comprehension. Data that are too complex, or that pertain to areas not meriting priority attention, impede effective decisionmaking. . . . A process that attempts to deal with the near infinite number of potential budget issues, failing to distingush between their priorities, is bound to be ineffective (1977, p. 247).

Cost, Outcomes, and Performance Information

The amount of information needed for budgeting is not the only concern, however. Many questions are raised about the nature of information that is used as well. Information in three areas is particularly at issue: What are the costs of postsecondary education and how are they measured and used? What are the outcomes of postsecondary education, and how are they measured? How is performance measured? Each of these issues is discussed in greater depth elsewhere in this monograph. Here, discussion is confined to the nature of the controversies surrounding them.

Costs — Bacchetti has effectively summed up the conflict and controversy about the use of cost information in higher education:

> Analytically derived cost information is the most underestimated and therefore underused tool available to college and university administrators today. . . . Knowing what things cost . . . and then basing decisions on that cost information says more about the caliber of an institution's administration than practically anything else. On the other hand, analytically derived cost information is today the most overrated item on the agenda of those who seek to improve the administration of higher education. Animated by the belief that an alternative reduced to a number is somehow more reliably evaluated, advocates of cost analysis are prepared to

20

overlook the intangible nature of education. . . . This substitution of numbers for judgment is wrong in principle and wrong in application wherever it may be found (1977, p. 1).

Considerable progress has been made to develop procedures for determining *average* costs (Renkiewicz and Topping 1973; Topping 1974; and Ziemer, Young, and Topping 1971). Extensive work also has been done to assess the use of cost information in higher education (Adams, Hankins, and Schroeder 1978, vols. 1-4).

A number of these studies point to important limitations in the use of average costs. Average costs provide an estimate of costs for a specific level of activity. They do not reflect differences between operational costs that are fixed, regardless of the level of activity, and those that vary as the level of activity changes. Thus Hughes and Topping observe

that while historically derived cost data can and often do serve all four management functions — planning, budgeting, controlling, and evaluating — other costing approaches, namely the variable costing approach, would be more appropriate for the planning and budgeting functions (1977, p. 17).

Although that conclusion is reinforced by Robinson, Ray, and Turk (1977), Holmer and Broomfield suggest that procedures based on average cost can be useful in the allocation process. Though they intentionally avoided the use of historical-cost data to prevent perpetuation of historically developed inequities among Oregon state colleges and universities, they developed a system that "in its conceptual form has gained unanimous endorsement from the chief executives of all [institutions in the Oregon State System of Higher Education] as an acceptable vehicle for the rational and equitable allocation of resources in the state system" (1976, p. 5). Their approach relied on three premises:

the principle of equity (in which institutions are differently funded only in specific areas where documentable differences in resource requirements can be demonstrated); the principle of external standards (in which average cost indices are derived from analyses of comparable institutions throughout the nation); and the principle of institutional autonomy (in which line-item accountability in resource allocation is discouraged in order to allow fullest expression of institutional goals and priorities) (p. 3).

Even though cost analysis has been used in higher education throughout the twentieth century, the technique has not progressed beyond the average-cost method. "It is only in the last year or two," Hughes and Topping note, "that decision makers in higher education have seriously begun to examine alternatives to average historical unit costs" (1977, p. 17).

Another problem with the use of cost information in budgeting is that as cost information is aggregated, it begins to lose programmatic and decision relevance. Schmidtlein and Glenny point out:

> Budgets are rarely able to reflect the real costs of activities and detailed plans of operation. Real costs are difficult and expensive to determine. The complexities of separating marginal costs from average costs and allocating the costs of activities that have joint products result in the use of conventions to simplify budget estimating. These conventions make it difficult to trace a clear, simple link to costs (1977, p. 249).

Outcomes and Performance — Progress also has been made in the identification of the outcomes of postsecondary education, though this work is not as well developed or as widely recognized. Lenning et al. (1977) and Bowen (1977) have both comprehensively examined the outcomes and possible benefits of postsecondary education. In addition, procedures have been developed for measuring some of the more immediate outcomes of instructional and noninstructional programs (Micek, Service, and Lee 1975; Bower and Renkiewicz 1977). But significant problems remain. Few advances have been made in the formal use of outcomes information in budgeting, but interesting experiments are occurring at the University of Hawaii, in Rhode Island (Micek and Jones 1978), and in Tennessee (Bogue and Troutt 1977).

A major difficulty in the use of outcome information in budgeting is the time gap between the delivery of education and the occurrence of the outcomes (Peterson 1976). Current measurement procedures focus on the results that occur during or immediately after the educational experience. Yet many of the important outcomes of higher-education programs do not occur until much later. Sifting through the many interactive effects that occur over time presents measurement problems that are barely comprehended, let alone dealt with. For this reason, researchers and practitioners are studying with great interest the uses that can be made of new procedures and studies concerning longitudinal student-outcomes studies (Astin 1971; Wishart and Rossmann 1977; Bower and Renkiewicz 1977).

The use of outcomes information to measure performance is equally complex. Balderston gets to the heart of the problem:

> Universities are more attuned to their processes and their mechanisms than they are to their consequences. They customarily have much more exact measures of activity or size than they have of consequences or results.

It is easier to get them to say how many students they have than what the students have learned and how they have changed. It is easier to count the books written than to say which are of value. Even the moral commitments of universities are largely to process and mechanism and not to consequences or to agreed goals. . . . But as to philosophical ends, universities are designed to house enduring disagreements without breaking apart (1975, p. 3).

As interest heightens in measuring the outcomes and performance of higher education, institutions must not lose sight of the importance of process. In many ways, the process dimensions make universities what they are. Unfortunately, it is difficult to determine these dimensions with existing measurement instruments and to incorporate or even accommodate them in budgeting systems.

Evolution of Modern Budgeting

Budgeting, like other administrative activities in postsecondary education, has borrowed heavily from the practices of both private business and public administration. To better understand developing trends in postsecondary education budgeting today, it is helpful to review the evolution of budgeting in business and government. Our review focuses more on the development of public-sector budgeting practice than on corporate budgeting. This is in line with the wide belief that "the goals of higher education are more like those of politics than those of the corporation" (Fischer 1968, p. 442). This perception derives from the fact that typically, profit is not the principal goal in either public administration or college administration. Instead, college administrators, like their counterparts in the public sector, usually pursue obscure and often conflicting goals. Despite this ambiguity of purpose, however, there has been a definite trend during this century toward a more businesslike approach to budgeting in both public and college administration (Glenny 1976a, p. 8).

In this section, we review corporate budgeting practice, trace the history of budget reform in public administration, and try to illustrate the relevance of each postsecondary education. The section closes with a discussion of emerging factors in postsecondary education — factors that likely will lead to further changes in budgeting practice.

Business Budgeting

Texts on corporate financial management are fairly consistent in their treatment of budgeting. Invariably, one finds that the benefits and purposes of budgeting in business are related to planning, coordinating, and management control (Heckert and Willson 1955, p. 14; Bacon 1970, p. 2). Budgeting seems linked particularly to planning in industry. Hastings notes that budgeting helps to systematize planning and suggests that in fact, "one of the great advantages of the budgeting process is that it enforces a degree of coordinated planning" (1966, pp. 51-52). Both Hastings and Heckert and Willson observe that budgeting is valuable in communicating overall corporate goals to lower managerial echelons.

Anthony and Welsch (1974) have discussed three types of budgets that together constitute the master budget: the operating budget, the cash budget (which controls cash flow), and the capital-expenditure budget. The operating budget, which shows "planned operations for the forthcoming year including revenue [and] expenses" (p. 324), relates most directly to the types of postsecondary-education budgets we discuss. They note that in the corporate sector the operating budget often consists of two parts, a program budget and a responsibility budget. The program budget, used by top management, states the estimated revenues and costs of the major programs that the company plans to undertake during the year. The responsibility budget, on the other hand, is used as a control device. It states the performance that is expected of each manager. In some cases, Anthony and Welsch report, it may take the form of a variable budget, showing "the planned behavior of costs at various volume levels" (1974, p. 325). The appropriations type of operating budget, quite common in governmental budgeting, is little used in business (Heckert and Willson 1955, p. 47). The appropriations-type budget establishes spending limitations and is used most frequently in such nonproduction areas of business as advertising and research and development.

Although varying somewhat from setting to setting, the approach to developing budgets in business enterprises is fairly standard. Heiser identified six common steps, beginning with the specifications by top management of corporate objectives. The formulation of plans and lists of assumptions by each department head is the next step, followed by the amendment of plans and assumptions. Budget presentations to implement the reworked plans then are made to higher management, approval is granted, and a go-ahead signal is given (1959, p. 38).

Budget Approaches in Government

Schick observed that the governmental budget serves three principal purposes: it controls spending, it enables management of activities, and it determines objectives. He suggested that proposals for budget reform usually result from a belief that one of these three purposes is being emphasized at the expense of the others (1971, p. 3).

As Charles Beard observed over 60 years ago, budget reform in public administration "bears the imprint of the age in which it originated" (in Schick 1971, p. 3). Depending on prevailing preceptions of weaknesses in public administration, new ways to approach budget planning have been proposed throughout this century. As we review the several important phases, note how each era of reform tends to change the relationship between control, management, and planning. Frequently, these reforms amounted to adaptations of business budgeting practices and were made possible by the increasing professionalization of managers — both in business and government.

Schick describes three major eras of reform in public-administration budgeting (1966, p. 243). These eras are best known for their respective orientations — control, management, and planning.

The Executive Budget Movement — From about 1910 through 1935, virtually every state adopted some type of budget innovation that might be considered a part of the control-orientation era, or executive-budget movement. At the federal level, this movement took the form of the Budget and Accounting Act of 1921, which established the Bureau of the Budget. State-level reforms in this era had one thing in common — they created or reinforced a strong role for the governor in developing the state budget. Prior to this time, the typical practice was for each state agency to submit its budget proposal directly to the legislature, according to its own accounting conventions and formats. Then each agency bargained directly with the legislative appropriations committee. Little attention was given to matching expenditures with revenues, and there was little interest in creating state policy to standardize spending in certain areas. About the only supervision received by the agencies was that provided by the auditor (Schick 1971, p. 14).

Despite the chaotic image that this scenario evokes today, it apparently did not present much of a problem during the days of smaller-scale governmental activity. When government did begin to grow, however, concern developed that public affairs should be managed more efficiently. In many states, citizen advisory committees were created to study budgetary and administrative reform. Frequently, their members were drawn from the ranks of corporate executives.

Observing public budgetary practice and drawing on their corporate experiences, the advisory committees proposed a series of reforms that came to be known as the executive-budget movement. Schick reports that there were at least three conceptions of the executive budget: as a means by which (1) the chief executive considered the needs of the state in its entirety; (2) the executive standardized and consolidated agency estimates to insure the efficient conduct of public business; and (3) central controls were exercised to deter wasteful or unlawful administrative behavior (1971, pp. 15-16). This third conception of the executive budget movement also led to the development of various uniform administrative procedures, including those for accounting, purchasing, and personnel.

Performance Budgeting — Over time, interest began to shift from use of the budget as an instrument of expenditure control to its use as a means of promoting effective management of public activities. This need developed, at least in part, from the greatly increased scope of governmental activity, with its New Deal projects, World War II, and the various post-war economic-recovery programs. Howard characterized the period from about 1940 to the late 1960s as the "management era," in which the stress in public budgeting was placed on output (1972, p. 49). This management orientation gave birth to a new budget-planning approach — performance budgeting. Although the 1949 Hoover Commission was the first to use the term, Schick notes that "the Commission coined the name; it did not invent the concept" (1971, p. 30). Performance budgeting was no more than what had long been known either as activity or functional budgeting.

Mosher states that "the central idea of the performance budget . . . is that the budget process be focused on programs and functions — that is, accomplishments to be achieved, work to be done" (1954, p. 79). In other words, activities were treated as ends in themselves. The typical performance budget comprised activity classification, performance measurements, and performance reports.

The activity classifications normally described the work to be done within distinct operating units and thus followed normal organizational lines. Schick notes that "the basic format of all performance measurements is the relation of inputs to outputs" and that performance reports are "a special type of performance measurement, retrospective assessments of what was accomplished with budgeted resources" (1971, pp. 47-48). Together, the three components constitute the management orientation of performance budgeting. They compare the actual work done with performance targets in individual work centers. The performance reports, by depicting deviations from expected performance, identify needed management action.

Planning, Programming, and Budgeting Systems — Performance budgeting hardly had been named when the planning orientation began to dominate in public-administration budgeting. The increased interest in planning, accompanied by new economic theories and a greatly enhanced ability to analyze and assimilate data with computers, led to the development of planning, programming, and budgeting systems (PPBS) in public administration.

PPBS had its origins in the Rand Corporation's efforts to analyze military spending. When Robert McNamara was appointed Secretary of Defense, he implemented this approach throughout the Department. Reports of success in the Department of Defense prompted President Johnson to issue an Executive Order in 1965 that directed all federal agencies to implement the PPBS approach to budget planning. Merewitz and Sosnick report that "the U.S. government quietly abandoned its compulsive version" of PPBS in June 1971, after it failed to achieve its promise (1971, p. 301). In more recent years, another version of planning-oriented budgeting has emerged — zero-base budgeting. It and the other methods we have mentioned are described in greater detail in the next chapter.

To sum up, we have witnessed three fairly distinct budget eras in this century. The executive-budget movement stressed control in response to widespread perceptions of waste and inefficiency in government. The performance-budgeting era emphasized management, drawing on such scientific management techniques as work measurement and cost accounting. More recently, the PPBS era has shifted the focus to planning, in the belief that activities should be more closely related to objectives.

Budgetary Practice in Postsecondary Education

Very little has been recorded about the approaches to budget planning in early American higher education. The late James Conant memorably expressed Harvard's long-standing philosophy and perhaps that of other private institutions of his day: "Every tub stands on its own bottom, each Dean balances his own budget" (quoted in Millett 1952, p. 230). But as Russell has since observed, state-controlled colleges and universities "have tended to model their practices largely on the experience in governmental service" (1954, p. 86).

Even today, one can observe aspects of each governmental budget reform era in postsecondary education practice. Many institutions still employ the position and line-item control tools of the executive-budget movement. Formulas that resemble performance-budget workload measurements remain common at the state level. And variations of PPBS or zero-base budgeting are the accepted practice at a large number of institutions and state agencies.

As a state moves from one budgeting era to another, it frequently just adds new budget requirements rather than replacing those already in existence. Thus it is possible to observe instances where the main features of an executive budget, performance budget, and program budget are woven together in a unique budgeting approach.

Since each of these generic approaches to budget-planning has developed to serve a different purpose (control, management, or planning), one would expect that budget planners at institutions in these states confront unduly complex requirements in their budget-development activities.

Despite the public-administration and business influences that promote more systematic budgetary practice in postsecondary education, one still finds much variety among the states. Practice varies in the public sector by comparison with the private sector, and within the public sector itself. In a seventeen-state study, Glenny observes that each state adopts its budget methods and practices "to reflect its particular political mores and structures" (1976a, p. 29). Glenny attempted to characterize each state's practice according to a taxonomic structure. Although the structure was kept purposely simple, he still found that "no two of our 17 states fit into the same cells in each column" (p. 34).

Although some current budget-planning practices were borrowed from the business world, financial management (and thus, budgeting) practices in postsecondary education differ from those used in business in several ways. To a much larger degree than is usually found in industry, higher education relies on fund accounting. Revenues are not pooled into a single account available for any worthwhile institutional purpose. Miller describes six separate funds that are established in most institutions. These are current funds, loan funds, endowment and other nonexpendable funds, annuity funds, plant funds, and agency funds. Additionally, each of these six fund groups may be divided into restricted and unrestricted funds (1967, p. 102). Governmental agencies, including state postsecondary education institutions, rely on fund accounting more of necessity than choice. These agencies are required to demonstrate that they are being good stewards, and they must account for the use of the publicly funded appropriation according to the accompanying fund designations. The approach to financial management taken in colleges and universities no doubt also derives in part from the signally important operational difference between higher education and business that we noted earlier — the lack of a profit motive.

Dunworth and Cook have observed that while the profit motive is the principal management concern in most commercial enterprises, no similar mechanism exists to influence management in universities (1976, p. 154). Moreover, other goals often are ambiguous and progress toward them difficult to measure. As a result, the budgeting process does not encompass the type of planning that takes place in a business enterprise to allow the manager to understand how his budget and activities contribute to the accomplishment of the organizational goal. As Morgan argues, the decoupling of goals and transactional data systems in colleges and universities, by comparison with the practice in profit organizations, "is not merely a matter of degree; it is a difference in kind that would require a quantum leap in theory to connect" (1978, p. 16).

Nonetheless, many budget reformers today attempt to use corporate economic models to develop public-sector budgetary schemes. The leaders of this movement toward the business model typically are legislators and trustees who attempt to apply their business backgrounds for the benefit of colleges and universities. Although sometimes admitting that their understanding of the links between the purposes and outcomes of postsecondary education remains rather crude, "they maintain that in due time refinements will bring us closer to the ideal of the economic or 'business' model" (Morgan 1978, pp. 13-14).

Emerging Issues for Postsecondary Education Budgeting

The lessons of history give us little reason to believe that budgeting practice has experienced its final reform. As the principal planning and controlling device in colleges and universities, the budget must continue to be responsive to emerging problems. Among the major tests that postsecondary education budgeting will face during the next decade are: (1) dealing with enrollment decline, (2) responding to new types of institutional activities (particularly those labeled adult and continuing education), (3) continuing to satisfy accountability demands, and (4) accommodating collective-bargaining growth. Additionally, inflation, particularly that related to increased utility charges, is likely to continue as a major budgetary problem (Ginsburg 1975, p. 45; Navin and Magura 1977, p. 216).

Enrollment Decline — The likely drop in overall enrollment in postsecondary education during the coming decade has been thoroughly chronicled. In Tucker's words, "alert managers in higher education have recognized for several years that their market was headed for a decline that may last for the rest of the century" (1978. p. 16). The enrollment decline, if one should occur, will have both visible and hidden impacts on college budgeting. The most obvious financial impact, of course, will be the loss of tuition revenues. Tuition charges may be increased somewhat to compensate for losses in income caused by lower enrollments. But Weathersby and Jackson, summarizing their review of several student-demand studies, conclude that colleges will encounter some degree of price elasticity in the student market (1975, p. 2). That is, increasing tuition may at some point trigger a disproportionately large drop in enrollment.

Potentially as threatening is the prospect for institutions in the public sector of losing state revenue as enrollments decline. As we discuss in the formula-budgeting section, most states rely to some degree on enrollment count in determining financial support. Although public elementary and secondary school systems have been funded through similar formula mechanisms during periods of enrollment decline, and Friedman observes that they have not felt the full, potential financial impact of their enrollment loss (1977, p. 84). This is because the formulas were adjusted to afford some degree of compensation. Widespread concern remains, however, that the coming enrollment decline will impact the state-funds portion of the college budget, since state governments now face both requests to support a broader array of social programs and demands that taxes be reduced.

A somewhat less obvious impact of the enrollment decline on the college budget will stem from the changed marketplace in which all colleges and universities will be operating. Even colleges experiencing growth will find that their ability to attract faculty and staff will be different than it would be in a pervasively growing market. Additionally, colleges are likely to find that they must allocate greater proportions of their budgets to admissions and program development efforts to attract new students and to remedial and developmental programs to retain students they do attract.

New Markets for Higher Education — As Tucker has suggested, schools can pursue one of two strategies to maintain their enrollment (1978, p. 16). Most of the comments in the preceding paragraph concerned his first option — obtaining a greater share of the existing market. However, many four-year schools are beginning to adopt the community college pattern and attempting to attract potential students not currently part of that market. In particular, there is growing interest in serving the adult learner through continuing education programs. But this new service opportunity alone may only partially ameliorate the potential budget problem. As Furman observes, "even though we will add adult enrollments in numbers beyond what we have in previous years, this will not offset the demographic projections for other major areas of enrollment" (1976, p. 7).

The move to serve new markets may even create other budget problems. Glenny speculates that one of the first decisions to be faced if adults are successfully recruited to the campuses will be who will pay the cost (1976b, p. 20). Many states have adopted a funding policy of subsidizing only credit instruction. Until recently, this would have excluded most continuing education activities, but now many public institutions are starting to award credit for such work. As a result, these students have become eligible for state funding through the normal formula processes. The incentive problems created by current funding mechanisms and concerns about maintaining academic quality suggest that this will continue as an issue for years to come.

Continuing Accountability Demands — The past decade has seen the term accountability assume many new meanings, and this trend is likely to continue through the coming decade. Traditionally, the term has almost always referred to the proper use of funds, although by 1972, Mortimer found it necessary to distinguish among management accountability, evaluation, and responsibility. He relates management accountability to organizational control, with expectations as to effectiveness and efficiency often being expressed in law. Evaluation tends to focus only on educational effectiveness and usually is an internal, rather than external, process. Responsibility is distinguished from accountability in that the former represents the assumption of a voluntary obligation, rather than a formal liability (1972, pp. 3-9).

Accountability demands have grown in recent years. Part of the growth can be traced to the creation of what Glenny terms the "many independent bodies at the 'proximate' level . . . [that] sequentially or simultaneously review the higher education budgets" (1976a, p. 6). The growth also derives from a change in focus. Adams, Hankins, and Schroeder observe that in recent years, "most discussions of accountability in postsecondary education have focused on the goals and priorities of the instructional, research and service functions" (1978, p. 74).

The past decade saw a shift from fiscal to program accountability; we are now beginning to see a shift toward social accountability. Neff speculates that this will be a significant problem in the years ahead, since most universities still make "particularly crucial decisions about resource allocation" that are influenced more by the traditional conceptions of the university's social role than the new demands (1971, pp. 116-117). For instance, Mortimer foresaw that "rising societal and legislative expectations and the rulings of the courts [would] be key factors in holding institutions accountable for providing equal access" (1972, p. 47). As postsecondary education becomes accountable to more groups for more purposes, accountability considerations in budgeting will undoubtedly increase.

Collective Bargaining — Another phenomenon of the past decade has been the advent of faculty collective bargaining. There are many theories as to why collective bargaining for faculty has only recently emerged after such a long history in private industry, in certain aspects of government, and even in some of the nonacademic components of the college. Some attribute it to the rapid enrollment growth of a decade ago, with a concomitant loss of a sense of community. Others claim that it is the result of enrollment decline and fears for job security. Regardless of the reasons, nearly every observer agrees that faculty collective bargaining influences budgeting.

Considerable attention has been given to whether the presence of collective bargaining influences salary levels of bargaining-unit members. Leslie and Hu reported that faculty compensation in unionized institutions during 1974-75 averaged about $1,291 more than in nonunionized institutions. After a period of steady gains for union members, however, this trend was reversed in 1975-76, when the advantage shrank to only $800 (1977, pp. 27-28). Naples and Caruthers report that "the traditional rewards — leaves, travel, bonuses, and discretionary salary increases for meritorious service — tend to be strictly limited by negotiated contracts" (1978, p. 9). McGown emphasizes this point: "Much of the budgeting decision making of today will pass to the bargaining table when formal collective bargaining begins" (1976, p. 14). And, in fact, Weinberg reports that in some instances, budgetary decisionmaking has shifted not only to the bargaining table, but to more centralized authorities as well (1976, p. 106).

Some writers suspect that collective bargaining influences budget planning even at nonunionized institutions. For instance, Leslie and Hu suggest that salaries are frequently raised in an effort to discourage faculty from seeking union affiliation (1977, p. 20). Other concessions affecting the budget probably have been or will be made in nonsalary areas as well. Regardless of the economic consequences for faculty, budget planning and decisionmaking consequences are real.

In reviewing the evolution of modern budgeting and its growing influence on budgeting practice in postsecondary education, we find good reason to believe that efforts toward more systematic budgeting are likely to continue at colleges and universities. Our survey of the budget-planning problems that seem likely to command most attention in the coming decade renews our convictions that more systematic budget-planning processes will be required to aid in their resolution. In the next section, we describe in some detail many of these formal budget-planning approaches and assess their potential for dealing with the problems of the next decade.

Analysis of Current Budgeting Approaches
In Postsecondary Education

The several approaches used in postsecondary education for budgeting have been categorized in various ways. Robins identifies line-item budgets, program budgets, incremental budgets, zero-base budgets, and formula-based budgets (1973, p. 10). The 1973 Annual Report of the SMU Institute of Technology (1973, pp. 2-8) identifies such approaches as: "every tub on its own bottom"; the "king's decree"; the "squeaky wheel gets the grease"; the formula; the planning, programming, and budgeting system; and zero-base budgeting. Bacchetti adds convergence budgeting to this same list of techniques (1978, pp. 3-16). Adams, Hankins, and Schroeder discuss "innovative" budgeting techniques, such as cost-income budgeting, internal pricing, and program budgeting, in addition to considering the more traditional incrementation of the previous-object or line-item budget (1978, p. 54). We find that incremental budgeting; formula budgeting; planning programming, and budget systems; zero-base budgeting; and performance budgeting are representative of the most frequently discussed and practiced methods today. Each of these approaches is described below in greater detail.

Several factors influence the adoption of a specific budget-planning approach (or blend of approaches) in a given situation. Baldwin believes that "budgeting techniques in use today depend heavily on the type of management philosophy being used within the institution" (1978, p. 3). Perhaps an equally important factor is the economic condition facing the institution or state. For instance, zero-base budgeting has been attempted more often in periods of sharp fiscal cutback than in eras of growth. As the five budget-planning methods are described, factors that influence their selection will be considered.

It is important to remember that each of the budget-planning approaches we describe is really a decisionmaking approach. Thus the line-item budget is not discussed separately, since it is a document for use in budget management and control. A typical line-item budget specifies objects of expenditure such as salaries and travel, separately for each department or budget unit (NACUBO 1974, p. 160). While the term line-item budget occasionally has been used almost synonymously with incremental budgeting, line-item budgets result from any bugdet-planning approach, since the control aspects of budgeting can seldom be ignored. Likewise, we do not describe the "every tub on its own bottom" concept, because it fosters very little budget planning; instead, it relies on a more haphazard process for institutional development that greatly depends on the fund-raising abilities of the various departments.

Incremental Budgeting

Incremental budgeting is the oldest budget-building approach of the five that we discuss. It was described in the literature at least as early as 1922 (Arnett 1922, p. 78-79). Despite the growth implications of its name, this approach can be used in either an incremental or a decremental fashion. While budget increments result from any budget planning approach, our use of the term *incremental budgeting* is restricted to a particular type of budgetary analysis and decision-making.

Definition — In incremental budgeting, each line item is either considered for an increment or remains unadjusted in the base. Frequently, increments are calculated as uniform percentage adjustments for every line item or group of line items. "Five-percent budgeting" is a well-established practice in industry, government, and higher education. The basic philosophy is that the current budget is distributed properly among both the functions and objects of expenditures and that little programmatic change needs to occur (Lawrence and Service 1977, p. 37; NACUBO 1974, p. 159). This is not to say that colleges following the incremental-budgeting approach do not make financial adjustments for shifts in institutional priorities. When such adjustments are made, however, they typically are the result of an ad-hoc determination concerning what increment is needed to effect the programmatic change.

Characteristics — During the past several decades of rational budget reform, incremental budgeting has acquired a bad name in some circles. The term conjures notions of nonrigorous decisionmaking or just plain laziness. Nonetheless, Adams, Hankins, and Schroeder (1978, p. 54), among others, remind us that it is still probably the most frequently used budgeting method in colleges and universities today.

Incremental budgeting approaches vary significantly. The "squeaky wheel" method relies almost exclusively on campus politics and invites bureaucratic infighting. The "king's decree" approach, on the other hand, is a comparatively closed process and may build either on a carefully developed set of the "king's" priorities or just his current fancy. At its best, incremental (or decremental) budgeting might resemble Stanford's relatively systematic convergence-budgeting method, which relies on extensive communication, trust, and allegiance to institutional goals (Bacchetti 1978, p. 18).

As budget planners have gained more experience with the newer methods, a greater appreciation for the advantages of the incremental budgeting approach has been restored, particularly as growth has diminished at most institutions. These institutions now face budgetary situations that offer little flexibility; indeed, they experience relatively fixed costs in staff, utilities, and maintenance. As a result, the most attractive budget-planning approach for them is the incremental method, where fixed costs of specific line items are adjusted for new price-level requirements and the residual sum, where one exists, is used to introduce longer-term corrections (Dressel and Simon 1976, p. 21; Reeves 1972, p. 1968). In some instances, schools that rely principally on incremental budgeting also use one of the so-called sophisticated approaches described below, in order to determine what to do with the residual. But most often, Wildavsky suggests, those budget planners tend to appraise the effeciveness of managers and reward the better ones. When there is a need to reduce budgets, they cut across the board and consider the degree of resulting argument to determine which cuts were too severe (1975, p. 5-6).

Evaluation — Much criticism of incremental budgeting can be inferred from review of the writings of those who are proponents for the so-called more rational budget planning approaches. For instance, Stonich notes that incremental budgeting starts from the existing base rather than from a clean slate and that it examines cost and benefits only for new activities. That is, incremental budgeting "starts with dollars" rather than using the purposes and activities of the organization as the beginning point. Frequently, he says, incremental budgeting does not examine new ways of operating as an integral part of the budget planning process (1977, p. 3). In short, incremental budgeting is considered largely as a financial exercise and creates only minimal demands for the attention of planners and managers.

In many ways, incremental budgeting is the most attractive technical and political approach to budget planning of the methods considered. From the technical perspective, it usually requires the least work and analysis. Politically, it causes the least conflict, since most budget participants implicitly assume that each agency or unit will receive at least as much on which to operate next year as they received for the current period (Wildavsky 1975, p. 329). Incremental budgeting may be the most widely used approach, simply because it works best. It implicitly recognizes the relative lack of flexibility budget planners in postsecondary education face, it is relatively efficient, and it is attractive politically. Its principal drawback is that it provides the least information concerning whether the budgetary decisions support institutional goals.

Formula Budgeting

Formula budgeting is frequently discussed in public postsecondary education finance and planning circles today; however, formula budgeting does not always enjoy a common meaning in its application. While the majority of the abstract definitions are fairly comparable, most assessments are based on an individual's experience with a specific formula. In consequence, it is difficult to describe formula budgeting in a generic sense.

Definition — The National Association of College and University Business Officers (NACUBO) defines formula budgeting simply as "the technique by which the financial needs or operating requirements of an educational institution may be determined through the application of a formula" (1974, p. 157). Hale and Rawson observe that the definition of a statewide higher education funding formula "is constructed to serve the esoteric purposes of its use" (1976, p. 18). Miller has offered perhaps the most widely used definition: "Formula budgeting is an objective procedure for estimating the future budgetary requirements of an institution by manipulating data about future programs and by utilizing relationships between programs and cost" (1964, p. 6).

Caruthers has questioned Miller's assertion that a formula is objective, arguing that actually a formula only represents a subjective judgment expressed in mathematical terms (1977, p. 4). Meisinger sees a formula as "a combination of technical judgments and political agreements" (1976, p. 2). In this regard, the formula may be little more than the "personal work procedures" that Wildavsky observed being used to simplify and reduce budget calculations in the federal government (1974, p. 147). Caruthers does observe, however, that formulas begin "to be regarded as an objective evaluation . . . when applied over a long period of time in a relatively mechanical way" (1977, p. 4).

Several writers attribute the formal beginning of formula budgeting to the California faculty-staffing formula in the early 1950s (Moss

38

and Gaither 1976, p. 544; Hale and Rawson 1976, p. 20). However, the concepts underlying formula budgeting most frequently are attributed to the pioneer work of Trevor Arnett (1922, pp. 102-4) and several members (Floyd Reeves, John Dale Russell, A. J. Brumbaugh) of the University of Chicago's University Survey Staff in the late 1920s and early 1930s. Examples of the latter effort can be found in Russell (1954, pp. 133-68) and Reeves (1927, pp. 248-61). This earlier work was basically a type of financial statement analysis in which ratios were developed for the various budgetary functions. Miller sees little real difference between cost analysis and funding formulas and believes that the apparent difference is only a matter of temporal perspective. "Cost analysis measures the past; formulas estimate the future" (1964, p. 6).

The lack of a commonly accepted definition and differences in terminology across states make it difficult to tell just how widely formula-budgeting processes are used. Gross found that 25 states were using some type of budget formula during the 1972-73, 1973-74, and 1973-75 budget periods (1973, p. 8). In reviewing Gross's study, Spence noted that of those 25 states, 12 were in the 14-state area of the Southern Regional Education Board (1978, p. 1). In some cases, the term *budget guidelines* is used in lieu of *budget formulas*. The use of the guidelines term most often indicates a greater degree of flexibility in the application of the ratios or formula factors (Kellogg 1974, p. 75). Using a definition that encompassed both formulas and guidelines, a Michigan Department of Education study found that "in almost every state quantitative guidelines and measures are part of a budgetary process" (1976, p. 15).

By far the most significant use of formulas is at the state level, where decisions are made on institution-wide bases. But there also has been some use of formulas in internal institutional budgeting. For example, Coleman and Bolte (1977) describe such work at Florida Technical University, and the Carnegie Commission mentions Stanford's "allocation-by-formula" policy under which the Graduate School of Business and the School of Medicine receive general university support by formula (1977, p. 102). Summarizing his empirically based study, Stuart concluded that university budgeting, like state-level budgeting, "can be moved in the direction of greater objectivity and equity through the selective application of various types of formula or cost-analysis techniques" (1966, p. 105-6).

Typologies — Of the several attempts to create a typology of formula-budgeting approaches, the most widely used is the two-part structure adopted from Boling (Miller 1964, p. 104). It consists of a

Figure 1. Example of Application of the Formula Approach to Budgeting

Enrollment Projection

	Semester Credit-Hour Production			Total Semester Credit-Hours				Full-Time Equivalent Enrollment
	Summer	Fall	Spring					
Lower Division	6,200	119,550	108,800	234,550	÷	30	=	7,818
Upper Division	16,300	113,250	103,650	233,200	÷	30	=	7,773
Graduate	15,100	24,600	24,350	64,050	÷	24	=	2,669
Projected Full-Year, Full-Time-Equivalent Enrollment								18,260

Full-Year Teaching Faculty Needs

	Enrollment		Student-Faculty Ratio		Full-Time Equivalent Teaching Positions		Recommended Annual Salary		Total Teaching Salaries
Lower Division	7,818	÷	28	=	279.2				
Upper Division	7,773	÷	20	=	388.7				
Graduate	2,669	÷	8	=	333.6				
All Levels	18,260	÷	18.2	=	1,001.5	×	$14,800		$14,822,200

40

Financial Needs

$14,822,200   +   33% for Other Instruction   = $19,713,526
Total Teaching Salaries   Expenses   Budget Base

		Budget Base
Resident Instruction	$19,713,526	Budget Base
Organized Activities Related to Instruction	394,271	2% of Base
General Administration	1,379,947	7% of Base
General Expense	1,379,947	7% of Base
Organized Research	1,971,353	10% of Base
Extension and Public Service	1,971,353	10% of Base
Library	1,379,947	7% of Base
Operation and Maintenance of Physical Plant	2,759,894	14% of Base
Total Educational and General Budget	$30,950,238	

Estimated Income

Revolving Funds	$10,292,785	33.3%
State-Appropriated Funds	$20,657,453	66.7%
Total Income	$30,950,238	100.0%

Reprinted from *College and University Business Administration*, Third Edition, by permission of the National Association of College and University Business Officers.

41

base-plus-percentage method and a functional approach. In the base-plus-percentage-type formula, the direct instructional expenditures of the institutions are defined to be the base expenditures, and the expenditures for other activities are dealt with as percentages of this base (Van Wijk and Levine 1969, p. 5). An example of this approach is shown in Figure 1 (NACUBO 1974, p. 165). The functional formula-budgeting approach calls for separate formulas to be determined for each of the functions. Each formula is based on a factor considered to be directly relevant to the activity, or function, to which it relates. For example, the instruction formula might be based on student credit hours, while support for physical-plant maintenance might rely on net assignable square feet. Miller maintains that although the functional approach is more complex in presentation than is the base-plus-percentage formula approach, it produces more reliable data for many budget planning purposes (1964, p. 107).

Halstead has attempted to classify all current formulas according to three computational methods, which he terms *workload* (or functional), *base* and *staffing pattern* (1974, p. 666). In its simplest form, the workload method estimates resource requirements by multiplying the planned level of activity within a function by expected unit costs. The base method first calculates the resource requirements for the base (usually instruction) and then the needs of other budget components are determined as a percentage of that base. The staffing-pattern approach estimates salary expenditures only. Using a salary schedule or average-salary target, total salary expenditures are derived after determining the number and type of positions required.

As part of a broader study, Wattenbarger and Starnes identified four general models of allocation patterns for community colleges, two of which may be considered formula approaches (1976, p. 15). Their unit-rate formula approach is similar to Halstead's workload method. They consider cost-based program funding as an advanced form of unit-rate formulas (1976, p. 17). Detailed cost studies are an integral part of this approach; in some instances, an institution's resource requirement is determined solely by a dollar-per-student criterion.

While the calculation method of the formula offers opportunities for useful typologies, formulas may be classified in other ways more valuable for potential users. For instance, it might be useful to know how the formulas treat different levels of instruction (student or course level or both), whether different disciplines are recognized, whether different types of institutions are recognized, whether the fixed and variable nature of costs is treated, and whether the factors are derived from actual experience or, instead, represent judgments about what relationships should be.

Characteristics — Nearly every publication on formula budgeting deals with advantages and disadvantages of this method of resource allocation. Some of the pros and cons are unique to specific types of formulas. As an example, unit-cost formulas have the advantage of simplicity, which aids effective communication. But the more complex function-based and workload-driven formulas are often considered to be more equitable (Caruthers 1977, p. 8). Certain advantages and disadvantages tend to characterize all types of formulas, although even these can vary greatly according to local practice.

One of the more frequently cited advantages is that formulas seem to provide for equitable treatment among institutions. Because they are quantitatively based, they seem more rational, more objective, in their approach to resource allocation. They are believed to promote effective communication between the institutions and state-level budget decisionmakers, particularly in providing financial incentives to support statewide priorities. Many argue that the use of budget formulas reduces the degree of inappropriate political decisionmaking, enabling campuses to retain a relative autonomy. (Note, however, that the disadvantages described in the next paragraph argue that nearly the reverse can also be true.) The fact that budget formulas can be used to predict resource allocations and can make decisionmaking routine also tends to minimize conflict among institutions and between the institutions and state budget-makers. (For an elaboration of these advantages, see Hummell and Spalding 1972, p. 30; Gross 1973, pp. 98-99; Hale and Rawson 1976, pp. 20-21; Van Wijk and Levine 1969, pp. 11-12; Moss and Gaither 1976, p. 553; Meisinger 1976, pp. 7-9).

Serious disadvantages are imputed to formula budgeting. Budgets derived with some formulas tend to improperly influence the incentive structure in several ways, particularly those formulas that discourage innovative practices; fail to fund start-up costs of new programs; encourage institutions to develop high-cost programs; or place undue emphasis on awarding "fundable" credits, regardless of qualitative standards or student attainment. Formulas are criticized because they do not establish levels of quality but instead perpetuate poor practices and funding levels of the past. A major problem envisioned for the coming decade is that most current formulas have an average-cost orientation and therefore do not deal with enrollment decline very well, since they were developed during periods of enrollment growth. A number of disadvantages have been cited that relate to improper use of formulas. In some cases, institutions have been expected to allocate internally according to the formula relationships, even though the formula was not developed for this purpose. This "superficial validity," to borrow Cope's term, also tends to make formula budgeting too rigid and unchanging when conditions dictate otherwise. A final limitation of formulas is that they are only useful for allocating within the higher education sector of state government. Although Halstead suggests otherwise, many believe that formulas do not justify resource needs for higher education against competing demands from other public functions (Gross 1973, pp. 98-99; Cope 1968, p. 5; Boutwell 1973, p. 42; Hale and Rawson 1976, pp. 21-22; Van Wijk and Levine 1969, pp. 11-12; Moss and Gaither 1976, pp. 553-54; Harris 1977, pp. 322-25; Halstead 1974, pp. 662-63).

Evaluation — Several attempts have been made to evaluate formulas and their use by states. Gross concluded that of the 25 state formulas he had reviewed, only 12 were acceptable according to his standards (1973, p. 97). These standards, which he developed with the assistance of a nine-member review panel, require that a formula (1) be clear, (2) be flexible, (3) not be used for detailed control, (4) recognize diversity of needs, (5) be equitable, (6) be broad-based and recognize the total operating needs, (7) recognize varying instructional costs by discipline and level, and (8) be objective (pp. 78-85). Among the 13 formulas judged unacceptable, these were the most common faults: (1) they were not flexible — that is, they did not allow special requests or were not modified frequently; (2) they were not broad-based — they did not consider needs in five separate functional areas, and (3) they failed to recognize varying instructional costs by discipline and/or level.

Greene, in discussing a functional formula-budgeting approach for physical-plant maintenance, listed seven criteria. Most of these are equally applicable to other functions of the institution as well: (1) availability of accurate data, (2) relationship between the data and the function, (3) comparability of data among institutions, (4) simplicity in communication with lay persons, (5) ability to treat equitably institutions of varying enrollment levels and (6) of varying degrees of maturity, and (7) ability to interface with existing budget management practices (1970, p. 58).

Criteria proposed by others involve a relationship to standards of quality rather than past experience (Summers 1975, p. 635), support of the statewide incentive structure (Stumph 1970, p. 226) and credibility when comparing the higher-education budgets with those of other state agencies (McGown 1976, p. 11).

In their present form, formulas are coming under increasing pressure, particularly because they cannot generate adequate resources during periods of enrollment decline. However, there is little reason to believe that formula budgeting will be abandoned in the near future. As recently as 1976, the president of a major state university claimed that a "formula system for making appropriations to higher education is essential" (Williams 1976, p. 4). Moss and Gaither determined that "despite its many weaknesses, no other method is available that meets so many of the physical requirements of the parties concerned" (1976, p. 560). None suggests, however, that formulas will be unchanging. Meisinger, for example, anticipates "the development of new formulas based on marginal cost differences" (1976, p. 225).

Planning, Programming, and Budgeting Systems

PPBS represents the third era in the budget reform movement. As we have seen, PPBS has been synonymous with the planning movement in governmental budgeting. PPBS has been legislated, established by executive order, implemented, discontinued, praised, ridiculed, evaluated, and feared. Most of all, perhaps, PPBS has been described in the literature.

Definition — As we might expect, PPBS does not enjoy a standard definition. It has been defined or described from a variety of perspectives. Kenworthy states that "program budgeting is a managerial technique designed to merge the planning process with the allocation of funds by making it impossible to allocate funds without planning" (1973, p. 19). Lawrence and Service describe PPBS as a variation of the incremental-budgeting approach, with reliance on analytical tools (1977, p. 37). The National Association of College and University Business Officers has defined program budgeting as "essentially a planning device that ultimately leads to a conventional departmental budget for operation and control" (1974, p. 158). Toler adds that "PPBS is first and foremost a planning technique" (1977, p. 3). Pyhrr describes PPBS as "basically a macro-economic, centralized, top-down policy and long range planning tool" (1973, p. 149).

The definition of PPBS we employ is similar to the one developed by the U.S. General Accounting Office. *Planning* involves the selection and identification of the overall long-range objectives of the organization and the systematic analysis of various courses of action in terms of relative costs and benefits. *Programming* requires decisions on the specific courses of action to be followed in carrying out planning decisions. *Budgeting* entails the translation of planning and programming decisions into specific financial plans (1968, pp. 10-11, 47-48, 53).

Morrell traced the origins of PPBS to the performance budget (1969, p. 286). He reported that researchers at the Rand Corporation began to apply the performance-budgeting technique in their analysis of military spending, and after many further studies and recommendations, PPBS was born. Commenting on the advent of PPBS, Schick stated that "the critical mass for change came from three sectors: economics, the new data sciences, and planning" (1971, p. 32). He particularly ascribed the method's development to the growing role of the economist in government and to the Keynesian influence on public-expenditure policy. In his Gaither lectures at the University of California, Hitch (then the Department of Defense controller) traced PPBS's first wide-scale implementation in the federal government. When he took office, Hitch found that military planning and budgeting were each already well established separately. But he determined that there was a need for programming "to provide a bridge between the two" (1967, p. 29). Because of the perceived successes with PPBS in the Department of Defense, President Johnson, through executive order, directed all the federal agencies to implement this approach. Over the next several years, many municipalities and state governments (and thus much of public higher education) followed suit. (For the interested reader, Merewitz and Sosnick (1971) provide more information concerning the early history of program budgeting.)

Postsecondary education was introduced to PPBS in a number of ways. Williams's *Planning for Effective Allocation in Universities* (1966) apparently was the first publication specifically discussing PPBS implementation in a higher-education environment (Adams, Hankins, and Schroeder 1978, p. 63). Many state-controlled institutions became involved with program budgeting through statewide implementation programs (Thompson 1971, p. 684). But numbers of other institutions determined that program budgeting might improve their own administration and implemented PPBS voluntarily in an effort to reverse the decline in public confidence and the ever-deepening fiscal crisis (Newton 1972, p. 1) for higher education.

Charactristics — In contrasting conventional budgeting methods with program budgets, Morrell found five characteristic differences.

46

The older methods were not output-oriented, focused more on the past than the future, did not clearly identify program choices, focused on resources requested rather than results, and did not suggest how resources were related to goals (1969, pp. 286-287). Using these differences as a framework, Morrell argued that program budgeting considers both inputs and outputs, places primary emphasis on the future, facilitates policy decisions, focuses on results, and illuminates the total costs of programs.

Schick identified four major changes that PPBS introduced into contemporary budgeting practice: the more explicit consideration of objectives in making budget choices; the consideration of multiyear rather than single-year costs; the analysis of alternative means of accomplishing the objectives; and an evaluation of the benefits or effectiveness of the budget choice (1971, p. 9). Fielden identified five basic components of a planning, programming, and budgeting system, in effect supplementing Schick's list. His principal addition was that PPBS take into consideration the effect of decisions on society (1973, p. 2).

The effect of the PPBS approach on traditional budget planning can be seen in the 10-step budgeting cycle specified by Parden (1971, pp. 203-8):

(1) Establish objectives and goals
(2) Develop alternative programs that will accomplish goals
(3) Establish resource requirements for each alternative
(4) Estimate benefits to be gained from each program alternative
(5) Develop an operating plan by selecting from among alternatives
(6) Test the long-range fiscal implication of the plan
(7) Compile the annual budget
(8) Evaluate the success with which program benefits are achieved
(9) Revise planning standards
(10) Repeat the cycle to accommodate changes and objectives, goals, available resources, and the institution's environment

PPBS in Higher Education — The postsecondary-education environment has placed further demands on PPBS. Dressel and Simon note that it is "not even clear what a program is at a departmental level," since most degree programs involve several departments in the use of general university resources (1976, p. 20). Morrell believes that the most difficult part of program budgeting in postsecondary education is measuring quality (1969, p. 289). Thompson fears that

PPBS may "lead in the direction of economically optimal yet potentially educationally unsound courses of action" (1971, p. 690).

Fielden observes that in a university setting, "the five concepts of the classic PPB have not remained intact in the rigorous formal PPB cycle. The internal political ethos of a university which makes it unable (and perhaps inadvisable) to seek common agreement on objectives, and thus measures of success, has removed the linchpin of the old PPBS" (1973, p. 5). Fielden suggests that the particular problem in setting objectives in higher education derived from the "basic inseparability of university activities" (1973, p. 3). As Fielden implies, this "joint cost" or "joint product" environment (in which, for instance, a single activity might serve instruction and research goals simultaneously) in fact presents more than just an objective-setting problem in PPBS implementation: it also impacts both cost and outcomes measurement.

Fielden proposes an alternative conceptualization, which he terms the "new PPBS," that emphasizes the need for participative planning in the university environment. Neff also has considered participation requirements. He maintains that for PPBS to be successfully institutionalized, it must become a part of the social and political makeup of the university. If PPBS responsibility is only tacked on as an ancillary unit of the institution, he feels that little change will result (1971, p. 119).

Peterson posed this question: "What are some of the potential internal impacts of PPBS on organizational processes, formal structures, academic policies, and social and individual behavior patterns?" (1971, p. 8). His own response was to hypothesize a number of changes that might occur in the university, including enlarged financial offices with broadened responsibilities, increased involvement of coordinating and governing boards in individual program decisions on individual campuses, and changes in the ways in which the campus deals with accrediting agencies. He observed that unless programs and subprograms were defined to be concomitant with the existing college and department structure, a strain on the existing framework might arise (1971, pp. 11-19).

Peterson's belief that programs and subprograms should be defined along organizational framework lines is a point of some contention in the literature. Wildavsky, for instance, considers program structures "the most pernicious aspect of PPBS," maintaining that "the structure turns out to be a sham that piles up meaningless data under vague categories" (1974, p. 203). Neff challenges both Peterson and Wildavsky. In contrast to Peterson, Neff argues that significant comparisons are not likely to be made and important questions are not likely to be highlighted "if the 'program' categories employed are existing departments and their current activities" (1971, p. 124). Unlike Wildavsky, Neff finds the program structure to be of great benefit, since there is a greater possibility "that the main conversation will center on the substance of the decisions and not on such undesirable consequences as petty rivalries, threats to empire building, and misunderstandings" (1971, p. 124).

The literature is replete with examples of institutionally defined planning, programming, and budgeting systems. The conjecture that the experience with PPBS in higher education would be different than that of the federal government has been borne out. In many cases, the literature reports a PPBS implementation in name only. Dressel and Simon concluded that with respect to pure PPBS implementation in institutions, "precious little has been done" (1976, p. 21).

Balderston and Weathersby have provided an extensive documentation of the University of California's experience with program budgeting from 1966 to 1971. They concluded that PPBS as a formal system had been "relied on only to a quite limited degree," both in internal resource-allocation decisionmaking and in relations with the state government in securing funds (1972, p. 299). Benacerraf et al. (1978) have described the results of a demonstration project to implement PPBS at Princeton University. While specific benefits from the process were recognized, such as "a greater awareness of the total cost of various University activities," the authors concluded that a total program-budgeting system was inappropriate for Princeton (1972, p. 387). The principal difficulties stemmed from the "great deal of time and effort" required to keep the system functioning (1972, p. 388).

A year later, Andrew reported an interesting variation then being attempted at the University of Utah. In building a PPBS system, they developed an analytical measurement called "enrichment analysis." Its purpose was to focus attention on long-range planning, setting objectives, and determining outputs during the budgeting process. Enrichment analysis was designed to communicate to deans and department chairpersons that the central administration wanted to recognize more than just enrollment in the resource-allocation process (1973, p. 5).

Kenworthy has challenged those who find program budgeting unsuited to small colleges. On the contrary, he found it "unusually well adapted to their needs." He believed the program budgeting procedures were much better suited to the normal governing structure of the small college than to that of the typical university (1973, p. 20).

Evaluation — As one might surmise from the preceding analysis, the evaluation of the success of PPBS toward improving budget planning in postsecondary education is mixed. The variety of evaluations derives at least partially from the variety of definitions. Although no unqualified successes have been reported, one does find opinion at the other end of the spectrum. Wildavsky states that "PPBS has failed everywhere and at all times. Nowhere has PPBS (1) been established and (2) influenced governmental decisions (3) according to its own principles" (1975, p. 363). Most other assessment is moderate. Raider, after comparing PPBS with other theories, challenged "the commonly accepted assertions that PPBS can improve planning, budgeting and decision making" in higher education (1975, p. 15). He observed, however, that postsecondary education lacks sufficient experience with the technique for him to conclude that PPBS has failed (1975, p. 1). Kershaw and Mood found that implementation of PPBS has been most valuable as a way of gaining a better understanding of university data bases. But they, too, noted infrequent implementation successes (1970, p. 343). Harvey judged PPBS to be "a failure as a system, but a success as a concept [that will produce] a positive residue of thought and action" (1977, p. 39).

Pyhrr, in developing his case for zero-base budgeting, asserted that there were five problems with PPBS. Two of his criticisms are particularly incisive — that "PPB focuses on what will be done, not how to do it" and that "PPB does not provide an operating tool for the line managers who implement the policy and program decisions" (1973, p. 149).

Indeed, the negative evaluation of many PPBS implementation attempts may derive from the fact that it became a parallel and competitive process to the traditional budgeting approach, rather than supplanting it. Evaluation of PPBS focusing on its ability to support (rather than replace) traditional budgeting is less common.

At the state level, Glenny found that most states "persist in adopting some form of budgeting which is called 'program' although the form differs dramatically from one state to another." He quotes the California state budget officer as observing that the states are continuing to move toward program budgeting, but at a pace slow enough so that it will neither "disrupt proven political and budgetary processes nor . . . extend themselves beyond the capacities to analyze what they have" (1976a, p. 29).

In *Budget Innovation in the States,* Schick closed with this assessment of PPBS: "If PPBS is an idea whose time has not quite come, it also is an idea that cannot be repressed by momentary setbacks" (1971, p. 218).

Zero-Base Budgeting

This decade has experienced yet another budget reform, one that has become widely discussed in the past several years. Zero-base budgeting (ZBB) continues in the rationalist line of procedures, although it is a microeconomic approach, designed to transform objectives into an efficient operating plan. This is in contrast with the PPBS macroeconomic orientation, or concern for broad policy decisions, and centralized, top-down approaches (Phyrr 1973, p. 153.). Although zero-base budgeting has achieved its greatest exposure since President Carter implemented it in the federal government, the concept has been around for a number of years. In fact, a principal leader in the ZBB movement states that "the concept is not new, but merely a formalization of the thought process" (Stonich 1977, p. 13).

Pyhrr is perhaps the best known ZBB proponent next to President Carter. He developed the current approach to ZBB at Texas Instruments in the late 1960s and attracted then Georgia Governor Carter's attention through an article about it in the *Harvard Business Review* (1970). Although there had been a ZBB implementation attempt in the U.S. Department of Agriculture in the early 1960s, Pyhrr claims that this effort "did not resemble [his] methodology used successfully both in industry and government" (1973, p. xi).

Description — Zero-base budgeting embodies a relatively simple concept. It demands a total rejustification of every activity from base zero, instead of incrementing the new on the old (Carter 1977, p. 24). According to NACUBO, the "zero-base budgeting technique assumes nothing about prior budgets but starts from zero each year to build a new budget" (1974, p. 160).

Despite the requirements of the theory, the governmental approach to ZBB might be more accurately characterized as "80%-Base Budgeting." Sarant finds that ZBB "complements and links the existing planning, budgeting, and review processes" and that the budget justification includes "selected, not all, current program elements starting somewhere in the base area [but] not necessarily at 'zero base' " (1978, p. 3).

Pyhrr finds only two basic steps in zero-base budgeting: (1) developing decision packages and then (2) ranking these packages (1973, p. 5). He describes a decision package as one that identifies a "discrete activity, function, or operation in a definitive manner for management evaluation and comparison with other activities." Each package includes the purpose or goals and objectives for the activity, the consequences of not performing the activity, measures of performance, a listing of alternative courses of action (different ways of performing the same function or different levels of effort for performing the function), and its costs and benefits (1973, p. 6). Generally, a decision package is prepared for the lowest organizational level, cost center, or budgeted unit within the enterprise. Each package is then ranked at successively higher administrative levels, with attention focused on those decisions representing marginal choices in terms of cost utility.

Characteristics — Stonich, an early worker with Pyhrr, writes that "the zero-base process pulls together a number of techniques that are already used for planning and control" (1977, p. 2). Among these techniques are many that we have described in earlier sections, including incremental analysis, goal setting, alternative analysis, cost-benefit analysis, performance measurement, and line-item budgeting. Stonich observes, however, that the strength of the zero-base approach is that it integrates these techniques within a systematic framework (1977, p. 2).

Both Stonich and Pyhrr have contrasted the ZBB approach with incremental budgeting and with PPBS. One difference is that the incremental approach examines the costs and benefits of new activities, while ZBB considers all activities. ZBB calls for constant examination of new approaches to job performance, while the incremental approach does not. Thus ZBB offers choices from among several levels of service and cost as compared to the incremental, take-it-or-leave-it budget (Stonich 1977, p. 3).

As we have noted, Pyhrr identified several problems with PPBS. He believes that ZBB can solve them and that the two systems are both compatible and mutually reinforcing: "The marriage of the two systems strengthens both, and PPB and zero-base budgeting can be merged into a coordinated process by changing the concept of budgeting in PPB into zero-base budgeting" (1973, p. 152).

Several investigators have speculated on what might be necessary for a successful ZBB implementation. Carter believes that budget planners must be "willing to work long hours to find out what is really going on and have the political courage to make tough decisions" (1977, p. 26). Cowen suggests that the system should be flexible and responsive to the particular needs of the organization (1977, p. 20). Pyhrr and Stonich both claim that top management must be committed to the process.

Evaluation — Like PPBS, ZBB has also received mixed evaluations. Carter states simply that "zero-base budgeting has proved its value" (1977, p. 26). Cowen quotes a municipal budget officer as stating that zero-base budgeting is a "practical impossibility" (1977, p. 19). Stonich provides a more credible evaluation through his survey of the experiences of ZBB users. Asked to rate ZBB as a process, 76 percent of the respondents said that it was either good or excellent for reallocating cost and manpower (1977, p. 15).

Postsecondary education has had limited experience with ZBB, although the recent implementation at MacMaster University has been widely reported. MacFarlane, MacMaster's assistant vice-president, has mixed experience. Included in his "good news" category were the gaining of much greater insight into the workings of the University, development of a tougher management approach, and achievement of cost reductions without excessive negative impact. His "bad news" included an unbelievable amount of paper work, tremendous amounts of time required, and difficulty in enunciating priorities (1976, pp. 31-32). However, MacFarlane reports that "once we used zero-base budgeting, there was absolutely no question by anyone that we would use it again for the next budgeting cycle" (1976, p. 32).

Gaither and Johnson suggest that the MacMaster University experience may be the exception because of its unique situation. At the time the approach was initiated, the University faced a $2.7 million deficit (1977, p. 11). Dressel and Simon claim that ZBB will have "little application in the university simply because so many of the commitments already made require continuing support" (1976, p. 21). If ZBB can be applied successfully in a higher-education environment, Gaither and Johnson think that it will be in the service and support areas, since these activities are characterized by greater flexibility in choosing the manner and level of service than are the academic areas (1977, p. 10). In fact, the implementation efforts in the University System of Georgia focused on these units (Fincher 1977, p. 55).

Morgan has yet to be convinced that ZBB will be useful to institutions of higher education, particularly at the more centralized decisionmaking levels. He believes that the viability of ZBB "is highly dependent upon satisfactory resolution of key theoretical issues" 1978, p. 7). Among these are criteria regarding the ordering of priorities, inputs to outputs, substantive vs. procedural rationality, and the viability of the economic or business model in nonmarket organizations (p. 7). He also expresses concern about ZBB's centralized pre-audit decisionmaking situation, which permits "top administrative and legislative officials to make managerial decisions fairly low in the organizational structure" (1978, p. 20). Morgan concludes that some form of program review would be a much more practical approach for achieving ZBB's goals in institutions of higher education (1978, p. 23).

Performance Budgeting

As we have observed, performance budgeting was the budget-planning product of the management era — the second stage in the development of public administration budget-planning practice. Although the emergence of performance budget is usually linked to the 1949 Hoover Commission, Schick claims that the commission merely "coined the name" and did not invent the concept (1971, p. 30). Its origins have been traced to the 1912 Taft Commission as well as to both the 1949 and 1955 Hoover Commission (Peterson 1977, p. 2). By providing performance budgeting with a label, the 1949 Commission did succeed in giving focus to the approach. This created a demand for improved federal budgeting and helped to develop a sense of excitement in public administrators of that era.

In more recent years, the term *performance budgeting* has again come into use. Peterson reported finding "embryonic developments" through his 1976 survey (1977, p. 3). Some observers, however, question whether this new era of performance budgeting is like that of the Hoover Commission. Many similarities can be recognized, but there are also many differences. If there is a difference between the old and new concepts, it is probably in the concept of performance itself. Whereas earlier usage seemed to stress quantitative workload, the concern now appears to be more qualitative and impact-oriented. Given the difficulties in assessing quality, even this distinction is problematic. For our purposes, further attempts at distinction probably would prove counterproductive. Just as there are many versions of formula budgeting, PPBS, and zero-base budgeting in actual practice, one should not be alarmed to discern several versions of performance budgeting in use.

The new growth in interest in performance budgeting is but one example of increased interest in postsecondary-education performance and accountability. A recent monograph is devoted to the topic (Folger 1977). In addition to performance budgeting, it addresses performance audits conducted by state legislatures (Berdahl 1977, pp. 35-65) and academic program review approaches employed by state higher-education agencies (Barak 1977, pp. 67-90) that affect the budget less directly.

Definition — Peterson has described performance budgeting both as *"a budgetary structure* that focuses on activities or functions . . . which produce results . . . and for which resources . . . are used" and *"a budgetary process* that attemps to allocate resources on the basis of anticipated or past results" (1977, p. 2). Schick sought to define performance budgeting by contrasting it with PPB. He wrote that "performance budgeting pertains to activities, not to objectives. Its principal thrust is to improve work efficiency by means of activity classifications and work/cost measurements" (1971, p. 8). He also observed that performance budgeting represents "a change in budget form" carrying the expectation that "modifications in budget form and technique will generate changes in the roles and decisions of the budget participants" (1971, p. 44).

The resurgence of interest in performance budgeting is attributed to various forces. Within the higher-education community, there is concern that current funding approaches emphasize quantity rather than quality (Harris 1977, p. 322; Peterson 1977, p. 4). Support for performance budgeting has also come from those who, in attempting to implement nontraditional or innovative programs, have felt stifled by input or activity-based budget approaches (Peterson 1976, p. 3). Peterson reports that, in addition, performance budgeting approaches are being considered by institutions faced with the need to discontinue ineffective and inefficient programs during periods of reduced resources (1976, p. 3).

There has also been renewed interest in performance budgeting among interests external to the institution. The Tennessee project takes the premise that allocating some portion of state funds on the basis of performance criteria will promote instructional effectiveness (Bogue and Troutt 1978, p. 1). Peterson traces the interest in performance funding and the increased concern for accountability to "the declining confidence in higher education, the size of the higher-education budget . . . and the pressures of recession and inflation" (1976, p. 3).

Characteristics — Noting that performance budgeting procedures had not been described in the literature in any comprehensive form, Schick developed a set of distinctive methods through analysis of current practices within government. He proposed that the common components of most performance budgeting systems were activity classifications, performance measurements, and performance reports (1971, p. 44). The performance measurements developed for each activity typically express the relation between its inputs and outputs. Performance reports, which were used as both interim-audit and post-audit procedures, compare actual experiences with budget projections (1971, p. 48).

Perhaps the biggest barrier to implementation of performance budgeting has been the difficulty in determining appropriate performance criteria. Three closely related "linking problems," in particular, appear to constitute the major obstacles. For instance, it often is difficult to attribute a particular performance or outcome to any single organizational unit, since more than one unit frequently contributes effort (Peterson 1977, p. 8). Similarly, Peterson suggests that "the linkage between outcomes and budget dollars may not be apparent" and that a cause-and-effect relationship cannot be demonstrated (1976, p. 12). The third difficulty is actually a variation of the second — the performance measurement cycle usually does not coincide with the budget planning cycle. Nonetheless, these rather formidable problems have not deterred interest in budget innovators. The subtitle of a paper by Bogue and Troutt — "Acting on the Possible While Awaiting Perfection — exemplifies this determination (1978).

Three state-level attempts at performance budgeting have recently been described. Peterson conducted case studies in the states of Hawaii and Washington (1977, pp. 9-29). While there were notable variations in practices between those two states, Peterson also found "striking similarities between the states, which reflect the obstacles to instituting a performance-based approach" (1977, p. 30). In both states, he found that the institutions and state agencies were still negotiating the appropriateness of certain measures and program structures, even though each state had several years of experience. Perhaps more significantly, he found that "performance budgeting lacks political appeal" (1977, p. 31). This assertion is based on his observations that legislators in both states (1) took a greater personal interest in defending the institutions in their own area rather than in supporting the supposedly more rational approach and (2) disliked the complexity and volume of materials to be reviewed.

The Tennessee experiment was instigated by the state coordinating agency rather than being mandated by the executive budget office or legislature. Its principal emphasis is on establishing and assessing instructional goals (Bogue and Troutt 1977, p. 107). The project anticipates the development at each institution of instructional performance indicators that are consistent with its role and mission. The coordinating agency hopes to use the indicators "as a basis for revising formula funding policies to reward performance" (1977, p. 106). Harris, a former member of the Tennessee project staff, has proposed a similar institutional funding scheme based on multiple-year planning and budgeting cycles. Under his proposal, the performance of the institution and its component programs would be evaluated by a board of visitors at the end of each cycle. Using this evaluation as a basis, a recommended budget for the next cycle would be prepared by central authorities (1977, p. 325).

Evaluation — While it is probably premature to evaluate the more recent performance-budgeting efforts, writers on public administration have assessed the earlier era as a failure. For instance, Lee and Johnson found "little evidence that performance budgeting ever became the basis upon which decisions were made" (1973, p. 107). Schick summarized: "Performance budgeting failed to achieve its aspirations and potential" (1971, p. 85). But as Lee and Johnson observe, "performance budgeting really did not disappear altogether . . . [it] continues, even though the popularity of the word 'program' in the 1960s all but buried 'performance' " (1973, p. 108). Schick, then, had been prophetic: "the disappointing career of this proposed reform did not deter a new generation of reformers from striving to convert the tradition-bound budget" (1971, p. 85).

The Prospect for Rational Budgeting

Although the foregoing discussion of the five budget planning approaches serve to highlight their differences, it is immediately apparent that several of the approaches have many common characteristics. To view these five techniques from a larger perspective, it may be useful to consider their theoretical and pragmatic similarities in addition to their differences.

The theoretical aspects of the budget planning approaches discussed above can be described in numerous ways. Three particularly important criteria for comparing these methods are their degree of integration in the overall long-range planning effort, their consideration of all rather than just expansion-based activities, and their concern for ultimate outcomes rather than process. Performance budgeting, PPBS, and ZBB tend to be similar in these respects. By design, these methods are integrated into the planning process, call for continual reassessment of the need for discrete programmatic activity, and lead to efforts to measure each program's performance. Formula budgeting and incremental budgeting, on the other hand, are similar in their pragmatic characteristics. They are designed to routinize decisionmaking, lead to more predictable results and minimize the paper work, conflict, and effort attending the other budget planning methodologies. The newer versions of performance budgeting, PPBS and ZBB, are products of the more recent planning era that increasingly demands reallocation and may be clearly distinguished in this regard from formula and incremental budgeting approaches.

We do not anticipate that the next few years will witness any slowing of the steady march toward rationality in budgeting. As we have observed, postsecondary education budgeting is heavily influenced by budgeting in government. If for no other reason, the move toward rationality in higher education budgeting will continue because the college is part of a larger enterprise. No amount of debate at professional meetings and no number of essays in higher education journals are likely to alter the fact that when it comes to selecting budget-planning approaches through which public institutions deal with state governments, higher-education leaders are not calling the shots.

This is not to suggest that all budget planners are like grooms at shotgun weddings when it comes to budget information. Chief budgeting officers in institutions of higher education, like their counterparts in government and industry, constantly seek ways to discharge their responsibilities more effectively. While recognizing imperfections or problems of various sorts in the newer budget-planning technologies, many still consider these approaches to be improvements on the older alternatives; and they are willing to experiment in pursuit of a more satisfactory approach. Some budget innovators in public-sector institutions may be opportunistic, merely riding with the tide. But this can scarcely explain the continuing innovative efforts at private institutions, where there is little incentive for change except the benefits of improved practice. We have viewed evidence of this in describing the PPBS efforts of small private colleges and the experiences of Princeton University. Certainly no government agency is forcing the University of Miami (Florida) to investigate zero-base budgeting. As new generations of postsecondary education administrators who have been trained in these techniques assume leadership roles, efforts toward innovative budgeting practice are likely to accelerate.

Beyond the influence of people in leadership positions, the demographic and economic realities of the next decade also are likely to demand continued emphasis on rational decisionmaking and, particularly, efforts toward what Morgan terms marginal-utility analysis (1978). While rendering good budgeting decisions has always been important, the projected downturn in enrollment, the increasing inflexibility of resources, and the eroding financial support base all combine to make decisions at the margin of utmost importance. Indeed, Glenny observes that some institutions of higher education that already face these conditions are now moving faster in budget reform than are state budget officers (1976a, pp. 30-31).

We do not necessarily believe that any of the five budget-planning approaches we have described come close to a final answer, and we expect to see other innovative ideas put forward in the coming years. The remediation of perceived deficiencies in the reform approaches (or some combination of the more favorable aspects of current methods) will likely provide the basis for such innovations. We are likely to see procedures that recognize the inflexibility of the base and that minimize paperwork and analysis (as does incremental budgeting), approaches that provide predictability and routinization of decisionmaking (as does formula budgeting), models that enable the rational evaluation of alternatives at the margin (as do PPBS and zero-base budgeting), and attempts to change the financial incentive structure through relating performance to the budgeting process (as does performance budgeting). No single approach is likely to emerge that embodies all of these characteristics, since there are conflicting goals among them. Nonetheless, these characteristics represent targets for future innovation efforts.

Budgetary Responsibilities
At Differing Organizational Levels

Budgeting provides a forum in which many actors can perform a range of roles. As Morgan observed, "participants play budgetary roles as their institutional position prescribes. Successful performance is determined by one's ability to make the best case for one's employing agency" (1978, p. 25). We come now to the identification of the various actors involved in the postsecondary education budgetary process and their multiple roles. Not all the actors are on stage, and not all perform the same roles throughout the budgetary process.

Roles

According to Wildavsky, roles "are the expectations of behavior attached to institutional positions" (1974, p. 160). Without understanding that the roles, or expectations, exist as a function of institutional position, one cannot understand the nature of the budgetary process. To emphasize the importance of performing in appropriate roles, Wildavsky cites the examples of the U.S. Weather Bureau, which at one time was exceedingly conservative in presenting its budgetary requests. During one appropriation cycle, the Weather Bureau found itself in the position of the college business officer quoted by Jellema: "The trouble is not with my budget. That works out well enough. The trouble is that when I get to the end of the budget, I still have a lot of calendar left" (1973, p. 63). Thus when appearing before the Appropriations Committee, the Weather Bureau official was chastised for being too conservative in his estimate of needed resources and was subjected to the following line of questioning:

Senator Smith:	Have you requested enough money to permit you to progress as fast as you can?
Weather Bureau Official:	Senator Smith, I wonder if there is any agency that ever gets enough money. There are always so many things you can do beyond the budget possibilities. Certainly we could use a great deal more. . . .
Senator Smith:	My question was prompted because we cannot know what you could use unless you tell us. . . . If you do not ask for it, the point is, the responsibility is yours, is it not? (Wildavsky 1974, p. 161).

From this perspective, the importance of advocacy in the budgetary process is apparent. Anton argues, for example, that an important role of budgeting is to "give the budgetary commission something to cut" (1975, p. 209) — which certainly does not suggest a conservative approach. However, other roles in the budgetary process are also implicit in the dialogue. The senator seemed to suggest that if sufficient funds had been requested, they would have been provided. But let us assume, for the moment, that the Weather Bureau had requested funds beyond what was available. In this circumstance, the senator would have been confronted with decisions relative to the requests of the Weather Bureau in relation to the requests of other agencies. No doubt he would have called on his staff to conduct analyses to provide some indication of the consequences of funding one agency versus another. Ultimately, the senator would probably have had to cut the budget request of the Weather Bureau. In turn, the Weather Bureau would have been forced to make choices about which activities to support at the reduced level of funding.

This example shows several roles that are necessary in the budgetary process: advocates, cutters, analysts, decisionmakers, providers, and expenders. These roles are not mutually exclusive and they are not necessarily on the same continuum. The same individual, as a function of one position, can be both an advocate and a cutter, either an analyst or a decisionmaker, and either a provider or an expender. In fact, the chief executive officer of the institution may play all of these roles.

The multiplicity of roles imposed on individuals derives from the two cycles of the budgetary process. On the one hand, the budget is used to put forth a case, to establish the need for and the desirability of the mission, purpose, and activities of the institution. On the other hand, the budget distributes available resources to support authorized purposes and activities during a given budgetary period. Depending on one's position, different roles are performed in each of these cycles.

Players

The more visible players are faculty, department chairpersons, deans, vice-presidents, chief executive officers, state postsecondary education officials, governors, and legislators. Less visible, though increasingly important, are students, institutional analysts, staffs of state agencies, and staffs of executive and legislative agencies. Glenny has emphasized the critical nature of staff work on important budget decisions, observing:

Much of the most telling leadership of public institutions of higher education today is anonymous. . . . Unknown by college and university faculties and students . . . [persons occupying these staff positions] are faceless, without names, and without the legal responsibility for the well-being of the colleges and universities. Nevertheless, as the state political leaders fail to see their goals of accountability and control achieved through the coordinating and the governing boards, they turn to the governor's budget office or the legislative analyst, or in some states both, in order to obtain their objectives (1972, p. 10, 18) .

The other invisible player is the student. Students, by choosing which institutions, or which programs within an institution, to enroll in, influence postsecondary education budgets. Some have argued that a free-market system should be adopted for postsecondary education, in which tuition would be set at the cost of providing instruction, and resources from governments would be provided directly to students. Through this mechanism, institutional budgets would be determined as a function of student enrollment (see, for example, Hansen and Weisbrod 1969; Hoenack and Norman 1974). Leslie and Johnson, on the other hand, argue that the "characteristics of higher education in no way approximate the sufficient conditions of the perfectly competitive market model. . . ." (p. 14) and "the market model is determined to be inapplicable or inappropriate to higher education. . ." (1974, p. 2). Though in recent years the trend in federal financing, and in some instances state financing, has been to provide relatively more resources to students than to institutions, it is unlikely that higher education financing and budgeting will in the immediate future be based on full-cost tuition. Nonetheless, students continue to exercise choices and influence institutional budgetmaking. As a consequence, the choices of students as represented in tuition income must necessarily be reflected in the budgetary process.

In the remainder of this section, we describe the budget request and budget allocation cycles as they relate to the educational and general fund and explore issues surrounding participation in these cycles.

The Budget-Request Cycle

As we observed at the outset, the budget is used to request funds and to allocate available funds among competing alternatives. Although many allocation decisions are implicitly made in the process of requesting funds, for purposes of this discussion we consider the request cycle to culminate in the appropriation of funds by the legislature and the allocation cycle to proceed thereafter.[1] It follows, therefore, that we are concerned primarily with the public sector in postsecondary education.

Most of the literature focuses on the budget-request cycle. This is understandable because, particularly in public institutions, most of the debate, analysis, and decisions are made in the request cycle. Campus or state-agency budget hearings rarely are reconvened to determine the allocation of appropriated funds. This is partially a timing issue. In many states, the appropriation may not be set until after the fiscal year begins. As a consequence, allocation must occur rapidly to prevent disruption of the academic cycle (Schmidtlein and Glenny 1977, p. 181). In addition, the intense effort put into the request cycle also tends to mitigate the need for prolonged deliberations in the allocation cycle.

Preparing the Budget Request

In its simplest form, a budget consists of an expenditure and revenue plan that will support the overall educational objectives and plan of the institution (Corbally 1962, p. 167). This description, however, conceals the many aspects and subprocesses involved in the development of an institutional budget. Robins points out that "the process by which a budget document is created is cyclical in nature. It has no beginning or end. It is continuous and overlapping" (1973, p. 18). He describes the preparation of an institutional budget as occurring in three phases.

In the "long-range planning" phase, which is not time-bound, the institution is concerned with developing or reassessing institutional goals, the demographics and environmental factors affecting the institution (such as faculty loads, tenure policies, the composition of the student body, the condition of the library and its services, the status of the physical plant, the overall financial situation of the institution related to its tuition charges, investment program, and so forth). One of the final steps in the long-range planning process is the projection of enrollment for the budget year in question.

---

[1]This distinction is relevant only to institutions in the public sectors and may be a source of confusion to those more accustomed to budgeting in private institutions. While many of the procedures may be similar — for example, the use of budget protocols or guidelines developed by central administration, the involvement of budgetary committees, and the casting of the budget in the context of overall institutional goals and plans — the separation into two cycles is particularly misleading. In private institutions, the budget-planning process tends to be more revenue-driven, with requests and allocations handled simultaneously and the distinction between the two much less visible (Cuthbertson 1959; McConnell 1967).

The institution is then ready to move to the second phase, which is concerned with program planning. Normally this phase begins about 18 months before the expected effective date of the budget. It focuses on the assessment and planning of academic programs, the planning of support programs, estimating revenue, and reviewing and revising plans and estimates based on comparison of estimated revenues with expenditures required by the educational plan.

The final phase of the budget process concerns document preparation and usually begins nine to 12 months prior to the effective date of the budget. It is in this phase that the formal request budget is developed. Many of the major decisions have already been made in earlier phases and are issued as guidelines for the development of the formal request budget. Nonetheless, contention and negotiation continue throughout the preparation of the final request budget.

From this description of the budgetary process, we can see that the institution is simultaneously engaged in different phases of preparation for different budget years. Long-range planning is being carried out for one year, and the institution is completing the final document for the most immediate budget year — all at the same time. This leads to confusion on the part of participants and also has created some confusion in the literature. Is budgeting, for example, top-down, or bottom-up? While arguments are made on both sides of this issue, if one accepts the description of the budget cycle provided above, the answer is that budgeting is both top-down and bottom-up. As a result of the long-range planning phase and, to a limited extent, the program planning phase, budget guidelines, or "budget protocols," are developed. As Massey points out:

> These are written instruments for promulgating general budget and planning information and providing top-down prompting to elicit bottom-up response to specific questions. . . . Protocols provide an impetus to plan more effectively at the local level and share these plans and their rationale with the central administration (1978, p. 363).

These protocols help to mold the shape of the budget as it is developed.

This is not to suggest, however, that all decisions are made at the top. As Masters and Munsterman observe, the budget normally flows from the bottom up, with guidance and assistance from the top down. They add:

> The budgeting unit in educational institutions is the department and it is very important that the responsibility for conducting the affairs of the

> budgeting unit be placed in a single individual and that individual is the department head. The department head is in a position to best know the needs of the department and the proper balance which must be effected in any allocation of funds (1975, p. 1).

Typically, therefore, the budget request proceeds from the bottom up, based on basic constraints, priorities, and planning assumptions (budget protocols) passed down by the central administration.

Several issues related to timing also cause confusion and problems in the budget cycle. Turrisi points to a dilemma in Florida that is typical for institutions in other states on an annual budget cycle. The operational unit of the academic area, Turrisi notes, is the department. The need to know about available resources is greatest at this level. Yet "department chairpersons are the last to know what resources they will have for the year which is already one-fourth gone by the time they find out" (1978, p. 1). And frequently, important allocation decisions are made in August, when the operating managers (department chairpersons) are out. This situation, which is a consequence of the lengthy budget process and the fact that higher education in most states is the last appropriation item handled, induces frustration and uncertainty at all levels of the institution (Turrisi 1978).

Why, one wonders, is higher education one of the last appropriation items dealt with at the state level? State governments, like the federal government, have increasingly assumed budgetary obligations that are of an entitlement nature. This means that the basis for funding many programs is defined in the statutes, and the level of resources that will be provided to different programs supported by the state is a function of the volume that can be justified for each program. In most states, for example, funding for elementary and secondary education is heavily influenced by tax equalization formulas written into statutes. Similarly, appropriations for welfare, transportation, and highways are largely determined by requirements to match federal grants, by statute-based funding formulas, or restricted tax revenue (such as a gasoline tax). Mental-health programs, prisons, and debt maintenance also are continuing obligations that usually take priority. The next result is that higher education, which remains one of the largest budget items in most states, is treated on a discretionary basis. Indeed, higher education is one of the few remaining major programs over which the state has discretionary power. Thus appropriations for higher education are determined in part on the basis of the need described in the budget request and in part on the basis of what resources are available after other state-program commitments have been met. This phenomenon becomes increasingly important, and potentially forbidding, in the context of the demographic and potential enrollment problems and the likely severe revenue constraints expected to confront higher education in the next few years (Schmidtlein and Glenny 1977).

Timing problems are not unique to institutions, as Schmidtlein and Glenny point out. The time available for an analysis of budget requests by postsecondary education agencies, governors' executive offices, and legislative staffs is extremely limited. Problems in this regard led Schmidtlein and Glenny to conclude that

> annual, rather than biennial, budgeting generally appears to create more problems as a result of losing a longer time frame for institutional operational planning and a heavier procedural workload for state budget agencies, than it solves in increasing attentiveness to emerging problems (1977, p. 203).

The problem is particularly severe when states decide to change budget formats.

> New data and data structures often require the design of new data collection and accounting systems; such changes are very expensive. . . . One president noted that it took his campus three years to regain the full usefulness of its routine accounting information services after a state-mandated change in budgetary data requirements (1977, p. 183).

The development of a budget in higher education is therefore a lengthy process. It is complicated by uncertainty, overlapping activities, and, in spite of the length of the process, difficult timing problems. It is continuous, with no apparent beginning and an unforeseeable end. Nevertheless, it endures and is the process by which postsecondary education obtains the resources that enable it to endure.

Constructing the Institutional Budget

Typically, institutional budget preparation begins at the departmental level because it is through the department and organization of departments that the university delivers its academic programs. In the traditional approach to budgeting, each department prepares its request on the basis of needed increments to continue to perform or expand its role within the institution. These increments may derive from such factors as anticipated enrollment increases, desires to decrease teaching load, or efforts to enhance the prestige of the institution. Breneman found that important distinguishing characteristics of different academic departments could be explained by considering them as "prestige-maximizing firms" (1971).

66

Dressel and Simon, however, argue that "as a general rule, inequities abound in departmental budgeting within the university" (1976, p. ix). This belief led Dressel to a series of studies (Dressel, Johnson, and Marcus 1970; Dressel and Faricy 1972; and Dressel and Simon 1976) that provide a comprehensive examination of departmental operations and budgeting. These studies brought Dressel and Simon to the conclusion that the traditional mode of simple incremental budgeting at the department level is no longer appropriate.

In the first study, Dressel et al. concluded that "the universities and departments within them are out of control" (1970, p. 232). In the second study, Dressel and Faricy concluded that

> most faculty members and departments seem to have operated on the principle that what is good for them is good for the university; and, in turn, the university seems to have operated on the principle that what is good for the university is good for society. But, in fact, what they perceive as good for the university is not necessarily needed by, wanted by, or good for society (1972, p. 184).

On the basis of this study, Dressel and Faricy asserted a need for planning and coordination at the state and national level. They also favored the introduction of constraints on departments that would be designed to make the students' educational experience more interesting and challenging, provide policies that students and the public would judge to be necessary and fair, encourage a more efficient use of resources, and encourage the evaluation of effectiveness on the basis of outcomes rather than on faculty and student preferences for process.

In the third study, Dressel and Simon examined the "problem of control of departments through budgetary procedures" (1976, p. 3). They concluded that budgetary procedures requiring the department to relate its activities and objectives to the goals and objectives of the total institution should be established, that procedures are needed to permit grouping of departments in terms of variables that provide an equitable basis for departmental funding, and that "a complete annual review and evaluation of each department and college is highly desirable and . . . should be planned in such a way that similar departments can be compared across the university" (1976, p. 112). They also describe several analytical techniques, such as clustering similar departments, that can be employed to better understand the functioning and contribution of the department within the university.

Though the traditional incremental, line-item approach is used in a majority of institutions, considerable pressure is building to adopt other approaches. Dressel and Simon effectively establish the case for internal purposes. But there are external pressures as well. Prescott, for example has maintained that "in spite of a growing awareness on the part of the university officials of the need for reforms in college and university budgeting, motives inspiring management innovation have been less a response to inner necessities of university management than they have been a response to the requirements of the external world, most notably, the state legislature and state coordinating agencies" (1972, p. 169). This observation is supported by Glenny, who comments that "state pressures for better and more comprehensive long-range planning are undoubtedly going to come from the politicians and will be directed at the state coordinating and planning boards" (1976b, p. 20). Accepting this as an environmental probability, Glenny goes on to maintain that

> an aggressive, realistic planning mode is the best defense against imposition from without of roles and programs for an individual institution. . . . State plans can then support strong institutional plans rather than initiate models and procedures for imposing state-conceived priorities (1976b, pp. 20-21).

Participants at Institutions

"On the matter of preparing a budget," writes Williams, "no magic is involved. Budgets are put together by department heads, deans and directors; analyzed and refined by appropriate vice-presidents; reviewed and commiserated over by university and college presidents; approved by governing boards; and then brought to the legislative group for study and action" (1976, p. 2). Simple as this process seems, it normally takes about 18 months, and there is much negotiation, and many conflict-ridden issues arise along the way. Though the preparation of the academic budget focuses on activities at the departmental level (Turrisi 1978; Lawrence and Service 1977; NACUBO 1974), the chief executive officer, the president, must retain the final responsibility for the development of the budget and for its transmission to the board of trustees. He is assisted by the budget officer, or perhaps the business vice-president, who administers the development of the budget by establishing procedures and formats, prepares decision packages, and manages the budget preparation process (NACUBO 1974). Though the academic vice-president and business vice-president play important roles in the development of final budget recommendations, it is the president who must finally resolve conflicts, whether between them or involving other service functions within the institution.

68

Final authority for budget approval, however, rests with the institution's board of trustees. The board must be assured that the budget represents and supports an educational plan consistent with the overall institutional goals. In the case of private institutions, the board must be assured that any proposed deficit is consistent with the overall long-range financial plan for the institution. The board should try to remain removed from the internal development of the budget, however. Matthews states that "it must be the president, not the board, who referees all the academic wrestling that goes on inside the institution at budget time. A board involved at this time will create chaos" (1976, p. 66).

The diffuse, participatory nature of educational budgeting is reflected in the 1966 *Statement on Government in Colleges and Universities,* jointly formulated by the American Council on Education, the Association of Governing Boards of Universities and Colleges, and the American Association of University Professors. The statement maintains that

> The allocation of resources among competing demands is central in the formal responsibility of the governing board, in the administrative authority of the president, and in the educational function of the faculty. Each component should therefore have a voice in the determination of short and long-range priorities, and each should receive appropriation analyses of past budgetary experience, reports on current budgets and expenditures, and short and long-range budgetary projections. The function of each component in budgetary matters should be understood by all; the allocation of authority will determine the flow of information and the scope of participation in decisions (AAUP 1976, p. 379).

To further clarify the faculty role in budgetary and salary matters, the AAUP adopted a formal policy on faculty participation (AAUP 1976). This statement argues for faculty participation in the preparation of the total institutional budget through an elected representative faculty committee, and for the development of criteria for salary raises and fringe-benefit policies that are "designed by a representative group of the faculty in concert with the administration" (p. 171). The policy statement further suggests that individual salary recommendations be initiated at the level of the department, school, or program, whichever is the smallest applicable unit of faculty government.

It is quite common for the president to use a budgetary committee in the development of the overall institutional budget (McConnell 1967; Kendrick 1965; NACUBO 1974). And it is equally common for the faculty, primarily through this committee, to significantly constrain the flexibility and choices of the president and the administration. Indeed, in those institutions where the faculty has much power, the president may be little more than a figurehead.[2]

In public institutions, as the budget moves beyond the institutional governing board, a variety of other participants become involved in the budgetary process. We turn then to an examination of the issues involved in the review of postsecondary education budgets.

State-Level Budget Review

Those usually involved in budget review at the state level are the staffs of state postsecondary education agencies, staffs of the governors' executive budget office, and legislative staff associated with authorizing or appropriations committees; however, the nature of their involvement and the extent of their participation in the budgetary process differs significantly from state to state (Glenny 1976b). Participation at the state level is a function of and is patterned after the distribution of authority for postsecondary education. In each state, this has evolved over time and continues to change, sometimes from year to year. Nonetheless, there are common issues and concerns among the states.

Most of these issues were identified by the study of state budgeting for higher education conducted by the Center for Research and Development of Higher Education at Berkeley and directed by Glenny. Glenny concluded that "no phenomenon found in studying state budget practice seems likely to have as much impact on colleges and universities as the growth in number, size, and professional capacity of the legislative budget staffs" (1976a, p. 98). This has led to increased redundancy in the budget-review function, increased competition among staffs, the imposition of additional budgetary requirements on institutions, and an erosion of the typical budgetary role of the postsecondary-education agency.

Redundant budget review is not necessarily bad. Our political system of checks and balances is a constitutional expression of the desirability of redundancy. Thus Dror holds that "the more critical a certain policy issue or one of its phases is, the more redundancy should be provided as a way to minimize the risk of mistakes" (1968, p. 21).

---

[2]We are indebted to Hans Jenny for this reminder of the real world. He pointed out that the quasi-legal "power without responsibility" that some faculties exercise in the budgetary process places a burden on the chief executive officer that he or she cannot fully cope with and, as a consequence, introduces difficult accountability issues.

The overlap of executive and legislative branches in the review function has on occasion approached 100 percent, however. If a state postsecondary education agency also is participating in the review of budgets, the problem created by the overlap is further exacerbated. Therefore "given the constitutional position of the executive and legislative functions, the coordinating agency's former monopoly on certain matters is taking third-party status in a two-party war." Glenny argues therefore that the state postsecondary education agency should move away from "its most prized function, budgeting," and direct more of its resources toward planning and policy studies, the development of information and management systems, program review, and an analysis of budgets in relation to long-range plans and policy analyses (1976a, pp. 143, 145).

Schick points out that "much discontent is a permanent part of the budget process, rooted in its bargaining/incremental mode, which requires the participants to play adversary roles and each to get less than he wants" (1971, pp. 167-68). This observation is reinforced by Anton, who stated that "recognizing the strength of built-in pressures (of operating agencies) to expand budgets then, and believing that these pressures will be reflected in budget requests, reviewing officials naturally see themselves as 'cutters'" (1972, p. 100). Taking into account the expectations that are associated with certain roles in the budgetary process, and given the inevitability of conflict in the budgetary process, can strategies be employed that help to minimize discontent?

Budgetary Strategies

Several strategies for enhancing budgetary performance are suggested in the literature. At the departmental level, Turrisi maintains that it is important for departments to justify their budget requests on the basis of the goals of their college; further up the line, the college should try to relate its goal to overall long-range institutional objectives and goals (1978). This should be done, Turrisi advises, not only in the context of the budget request but throughout the year as well. Effective communication between department heads and deans regarding needs and plans is likely to minimize confusion and misunderstandings at budget time.

Similarly, effective analysis can strengthen budgetary outcomes. Setting aside for the moment consideration of whether effective analysis provides insight and aids decisionmaking in budgeting, the mere existence of analytical backup lends credence to the legitimacy of the budget requests. The existence of analytical backup gives an impression of effective management and induces confidence among reviewing agencies and appropriation committees that the budget request is justified; thus, in this instance, form transcends substance.

Anton suggests four rules for preparing and submitting budgets:

(1) Avoid requests for sums smaller than the current appropriation.
(2) Put as much as possible of the new request (particularly items with top priority) into the basic budget.
(3) Increases that are desired should be made to appear small and should grow out of existing operations (the appearance of fundamental change should be avoided).
(4) Give the Budgetary Commission something to cut (1975, pp. 208-209).

A caution to these rules is provided, however, by Wildavsky: "If an agency continually submits requests far above what it actually gets, the budget bureau and the appropriations committee lose confidence in it and automatically cut large chunks before looking at the budget in detail" (1974, p. 21).

Research by Leloup and Moreland (1978) on budgetary success in federal agencies does not support this advice, however. Assertive agencies — those that ask for substantial increases in their budget — experienced larger cuts in the request (partially because their request was so great), but also received larger increments in the eventual appropriation than those agencies that made more modest requests. "The 'normal' strategy of moderation posited by the incremental theorists is more myth than reality," they write. "The strategy of moderation may be desirable for agencies seeking certainty, stability, and high support of their initial request, but it will not lead to agency growth and may in fact lead to agency decline" (p. 239). Assertive agencies are those than can generate public support or that have effective advocacy relationships in the executive or legislative branches. The key to budget growth, according to these authors, is to "attain a position of political support (with support inside and outside of government) to justify a large increase. 'Don't come in too high' is poor advice for an agency wishing to receive more money; 'come in as high as you can justify' would appear to be better advice based on the results of this study" (p. 239).

The need to be politically aware and to formulate budgetary strategies accordingly is reaffirmed by Schmidtlein and Glenny:

> Institutions clearly need to be more aware of the economic, demographic, political, and social context in which they are pursuing their budget

objectives; insensitivity to emerging trends will certainly create problems when formulating and defending budgets (1977, p. 202).

The budget-request cycle extends over a long period and involves many different participants and complex strategic considerations. Though there are no easy formulas for more successful participation in this cycle, we concur with Glenny's observation above, that the best defense is a good defense. To the extent that a departmental chairperson is able to articulate the objectives of the department, to explain how these objectives relate to the overall goals and directions of the institution, and to document the service provided by the department to the other departments in the institution, the budget-request cycle is likely to be less uncertain, less forbidding, and more rewarding. In spite of Anton's rules, a budget developed in this manner is likely to be more defensible and more successful than one that relies on the expectation of increments from funders. Such a strategy is not easy to implement, of course. It presumes that faculty, through their departments, will subscribe to institutional goals and that these goals coincide with environmental realities and are consistent with the postsecondary needs of the institution's service area. Nonetheless, unless the institution has developed a power base that can overcome analytically based processes, a well-reasoned and effectively documented budget justification is likely to be the best insurance for success in the budget-request cycle.

The Budget-Allocation Cycle

Reeves has observed:

> One of the persistent myths of academia is that every central administration has a secret fund which, like the widow's meal barrel that nourished the prophet Elijah, is both inexhaustable and self-replenishing. . . . Many faculty members and most students seem to have accepted this myth implicitly. . . . Unfortunately, this popular myth is the sheerest fantasy. The resources which come to an institution are indeed finite, often are severely limited, and never are sufficient to meet the accumulated demands upon them (1972, p. 167).

Frequently the amount of funds allocated to the institution reveals the nature of this fantasy.

The budget-request cycle ends when the legislature passes the appropriations bill for higher education. The nature of this bill varies considerably from state to state. In some states, the appropriations are provided directly to the institutions through the appropriation bill. In other states, they are provided to the systems which in turn allocate resources to institutions. In some states, they are allocated by the governor's executive budget office. And in other states, they are allocated through the state postsecondary education agency. Common to most states, however, are legislative directives attached to the appropriations bill.

Legislative Directives

These directives are frequently referred to as "riders." Through riders, the legislature evidences its interest in specific aspects of higher education. They take many forms. They may express an expectation regarding tuition charges. They frequently indicate specific programs that should be established or that are specifically not funded by the appropriation. They provide specific institutional or campus allocation targets for system appropriations. And they are used for a variety of other purposes. In Florida, for example, the 1976 appropriation bill for the universities contained more than 40 riders, dealing with such educational issues as the conduct of an enrollment-estimating conference, the naming of a building, the water rate to be paid to the City of Gainsville, identification of minimum allocations to be provided to legislatively favored projects, reinstitution of the "fact book" on higher education, and the development of a uniform information system (Florida Legislature 1978).

If during a particular legislative session a controversial issue emerges involving a program, an institution, a system, or the state postsecondary education agency, one result often is a rider to the appropriations bill that expresses legislative intent regarding the particular issue. The incidence of riders seems to be on the increase, and they are frequently regarded as invasions of institutional prerogatives. A particular source of frustration is the fact that in some states, the operation of the conference committee is such that riders are seldom debated in conference, not subjected to the scrutiny of the respective appropriations committee, and almost never questioned in final consideration by the full legislature. Indeed, riders often are the legislative equivalent of an executive fiat.

Execution of the Legislative Allocation

Once the appropriations bill is passed, the allocation process moves fairly rapidly. Though the governor's office is the formal executor of legislative appropriations, in most states the governor's executive budget office plays a relatively small role in this stage of the allocation process. If legislative appropriations are to be allocated to institutions through a state agency or a system office, some kind of formula allocation, based on workload estimates, is often used.

The nature of the formula and its foundations have normally been worked out in the request cycle. As a consequence, relatively little time is spent during the allocation cycle on reconsideration of the elements of the formula. Seldom, though, is there just a simple application of the formula to determine specific appropriations for institutions. Special riders in the appropriations bill must be considered. In addition, specific programmatic needs of institutions not sufficiently accommodated in the formula must be reviewed and considered with respect to their combined impact on and interaction with the formula allocations. If the allocations are from the state postsecondary education agency to system offices, relatively more emphasis is placed on the use of the formulas to determine the system allocation, on the assumption that the system offices will, in developing their specific institutional allocations, undertake to accommodate specific institutional needs and requirements.

Once the institution receives notification of its funding level, allocations must be made to colleges and departments and to other service functions within the institution. Turrisi describes the process in Florida — one that is used also in other states:

> The distribution process usually starts with the 'taking off the top' resources to fund mandated types of expenditures. These include such items as liability insurance, workman's compensation, Personnel Board fees, and, of course, the constantly increasing utility payments. Salary commitments for on-going personnel are considered during this phase also (1978, p. 6).

Reserve levels are also established to provide contingency against enrollment fluctuations that would cause tuition and fee revenue to be less than what was estimated in the budget.

The remainder is usually distributed to vice-presidents or college deans, depending on the organization of the institution, and "often with the participation of a Budget Committee" (Turrisi 1978, p. 6). From that point, resources are provided to the departments and service programs in line with an assessment of programmatic need, enrollment factors, and special requests for new programmatic activities, or by using an incremental approach based on last year's budget.

An interesting allocation model primarily used by, though conceptually not limited to, some private institutions is described by

Rogers and Van Horn. They describe a "profit center" decentralized resource-allocation system in which

> each profit center, school or department, earns income directly. This income is used by the subunit to pay its own direct operating expenses and to purchase from other areas of the university. . . .
>
> The benefits [of this model] generally lie in two areas. The first is a more informed . . . and more adaptive management structure. . . . The second advantage is the ability to provide more direct incentives for subunits (1977, p. 141).

Turrisi argues that "in theory, a reallocation of resources should occur and track enrollment shifts and priority changes; in practice, major reallocations of resources seldom occur" (1978, p. 9). She points out that about 75 percent of the university's funds is used for salaries and another 10 percent is devoted to uncontrollables such as utilities. Moreover, of the remaining 15 percent, a large portion must be used to provide base-level support for small programs or programs that are experiencing decreasing enrollment. The result, Turrisi maintains, is that "the reallocation of resources in the atmosphere of steady state or decreasing overall funding, therefore, is a slow and painful process" (1978, p. 9).

Recognizing the problems facing higher education in the future, the Carnegie Commission has nonetheless focused on the necessity of reallocation. The Commission recommends six strategies:

> Combinations of policies that will achieve this goal [reallocation] will vary from institution to institution but may well include elements of (1) selective cutbacks, (2) across-the-board budgetary cuts, (3) consolidation of existing programs, (4) readaption of existing programs, (5) 'every tub on its own bottom,' and (6) central reassignment of positions vacated due to resignation, retirement, or death (1972, p. 103).

By the time budget targets are finally provided to the individual departments, the fiscal year has probably already begun, and the beginning of the academic year is just around the corner. Turrisi points out that "these time frames are . . . totally out-of-step with decisions which must be made by the Chairperson if he or she is to manage his or her Department with any sort of responsibility" (1978, p. 7). It is not possible to wait until August to find out about the allocation of a new position and still find someone to fill that position by the beginning of the academic year. Similarly, graduate-student positions must be filled before final appropriation figures are obtained. Thus vice-presidents, deans, and department chairpersons frequently will take the risk that somehow the funds will be provided for these positions.

These timing problems produce frustration, confusion, and uncertainty, and necessitate a certain amount of risk-taking on the part of academic administrators. Add to this the inevitable conflict in the budgetary process, and it is easy to understand the tension that is part of budgeting in postsecondary education.

The Years Ahead

Postsecondary education will confront many difficult challenges in the years ahead. The costs of doing business are likely to continue to increase, making it more expensive for students to attend. Fewer high-school graduates will be available for enrollment in colleges and, as a consequence, institutions will try to find ways to serve other kinds of students. Competing demands for other social services combined with possible revenue reductions made by our increasingly tax-conscious society will make it more difficult to justify continued budget increases. Pressures for accountability and cost reduction are not likely to abate. As these pressures begin to be felt by individual faculty members, the trend toward collective bargaining in higher education can be expected to increase.

Budget Enrollments and Revenue

Perhaps the most pervasive of these forces that we believe will affect budgeting in postsecondary education is the predicted enrollment decline. Since an enrollment decline probably will mean budget decreases (at least when expressed in constant dollars), how might the budget planner respond? The most commonly predicted reaction is resource reallocation. But the claims of proponents of zero-base budgeting notwithstanding, American colleges for the most part have not yet had to make the large numbers of reallocation decisions that will be necessary if the projected enrollment reductions materialize. ZBB's discrete decision packages are unlikely, in themselves, to handle the budget stresses of the magnitude envisioned. Some technique that integrates planning and budgeting in a comprehensive sense, such as PPBS, most likely will emerge, since many schools will be forced to substantially change their institutional plans in such financial situations. The budget planner is also likely to reconsider the types of employment obligations that the institution accepts. Because salaries represent the biggest budgetary commitment at virtually all institutions, we expect to see much greater reliance on fixed-term appointments, part-time assignments, shared appointments, and perhaps even some type of productivity-based compensation plans.

New Markets

The new markets that institutions of higher education are entering represent at least a partial solution to this enrollment shortfall problem. But they also pose new kinds of planning and budgeting problems. We have described the dilemma the academic and financial planner faces in awarding academic credit for new forms of educational activity. On one hand, the budgeteer is tempted to consider such work equivalent to the college's existing program, so that it might be eligible for state funding; on the other hand, the budgeteer is nagged by concern that the academic enterprise will be undermined. Few schools have faced this problem on any appreciable scale so far. Of these that have, even fewer have come to grips with it in any comprehensive manner. Not surprisingly, the most likely solution again will be a closer linking of planning and budgeting, particularly that aspect of planning that seriously reevaluates an institution's mission and role. Interestingly, the personnel practices that may seem likely to accompany enrollment decline may also be of use here. This is because the inherent nature of the academic program in serving new markets (off-campus offerings, irregular program lengths, and the use of instructional personnel not traditionally qualified) directly conflicts with most current academic personnel policies.

Any prognostication entails uncertainty, but predicting the impacts of accountability on future budgeting practice is especially hazardous. Within 22 days during the summer of 1978, California academic and financial planners had two accountability reminders—the Bakke decision and Proposition 13. Though the direct impact of both was in a single state, there is little reason to doubt that higher education planners in all 50 states will have to contend with this kind of change in the social environment over the coming decade. Taken together, the Bakke decision and Proposition 13 place the postsecondary education administrator in a quandary. He is at once being asked to extend new services to new populations and to reduce programs by however much is necessary to live within a greatly reduced budget. It is tempting to hypothesize that one force or the other will have to give. A more realistic assessment, however, indicates that the program and budget planner will have to cope with both of these competing public accountability demands, and without specific policy guidance.

Collective Bargaining

There will be other conflicting pressures on the budget planner in the years ahead. The emergence of collective bargaining and the demands of employee groups probably will be in direct opposition to the types of personnel practices needed to be responsive to declining enrollments and new student markets. While these conditions call for the greatest flexibility possible in faculty and staff commitments, collective-bargaining agents will argue for greater job security. If this cloud has a silver lining, it is that collective bargaining enables the employer to deal with employees as a group. The very nature of a labor contract creates specific expectations of and obligations for employee as well as employer. For instance, the financial exigency dismissal of faculty members at the State University of New York several years ago was administered through a clause in the faculty employment contract. Another advantage of collective bargaining is that to be successful in negotiations, an organized faculty will need to be better informed about the financial condition of the institution and the implications of various plans of action.

Politics and Analysis

The complexity and conflict inherent in these issues assure us that there will be no easy resolutions. It is probable that enhanced analytical support for decisionmaking will be required and that budgeting will be concerned with value-laden problems. And so the debate surrounding the political and technical dimensions of budgeting, though frequently artificial and clothed in hyperbole, is not likely to diminish. Increasing demands for social accountability and the prospect of greatly changed college missions and roles will lead to vigorous politically based debate, both within and outside the institution. Similarly, significant resource allocation, the evaluation of the financial impact of serving new markets, and the negotiation of labor proposals will demand more sophisticated technical analysis. Both political negotiation and technical analysis and support will be 'mportant, therefore, and some decisionmakers will value one type over the other in reaching decisions.

Budgeting Theory and Reform

Since the development of a theory of budgeting is imbedded in the political-technical debate, the theory will continue to develop slowly. While it is usually agreed that development of techniques follows the development of theory, this may not be the case. Necessity being the mother of invention, we are likely to see many new budgeting techniques devised to deal with the emerging issues that we have discussed as well as with some we have not foreseen. Glenny observes that institutions are now pushing for budgetary change at a rate faster than state-level innovators can respond. With such new-found support for innovation, the coming decade may well experience a heightened pace of budget reform and a new age of acronymia.

If there was any lesson to be learned from our review of public-administration budgetary history, it was that reform takes a long time and that the broad reform has many manifestations in specific budget-planning approaches. Using Schick's framework to describe the control, management, and planning eras of budgeting, one must conclude that the planning era is still relatively young. If the quarter-century average life of both the control and the management eras is indicative of the life expectancy for the planning era, it is only half completed. Thus, to assert that PPBS is dead or that ZBB is already dying may be an example of not seeing the forest for the trees. We may well be in the middle of a much larger era that will come to be known for its marginal-utility analysis approaches to budgeting.

Thus far, we seem to be pointing to a conclusion that budgeting practice in postsecondary education is likely to undergo significant change. But how changed will it really be for the participants? Will the four points of contention that we have identified—participation, centralization, equity, and information—be enduring issues? We believe that indeed these concerns are enduring ones for postsecondary education budgeting, and that regardless of what the next several decades may bring, the debates about budgeting will sound familiar.

Participation

More than most other types of social organizations, colleges and universities have practiced a relatively participatory form of budgetary decisionmaking. And participation has always been a major source of contention within the educational enterprise. The next 20 years are likely to see this debate heightened. The complexity surrounding the college and its financial condition is becoming so great that it demands strong management. Decisions will need to be made more rapidly and with a greater singleness of purpose than most participatory forms permit. But at the same time, this complexity will require highly informed decisions, and a degree of insight that will not likely be found in a small, central, administrative team. The demand for collegial decisionmaking therefore will continue. Although the role of students in decisionmaking has been limited thus far, the impact of student choices is likely to become more dominant through the general condition of a buyer's (student's) market. The wishes of the consumer will likely be heard more frequently and more forcefully in the coming years. While it is difficult to determine which of these forces may prevail, it is fairly certain that concerns over the type and degree of wide-scale participation in budgetary decisionmaking will continue.

Centralization

Some state systems of higher education are already preparing for the enrollment squeeze of the 1980s through centralized master-planning efforts. They are trying to determine, from systemwide offices, which institutions have legitimate claims for which kinds of students, in the belief that only prior centralized planning will prevent outright war among institutions over students. But this type of action is coming at a time when many social observers are sensing a growing disenchantment with large government. Indeed, this has been a strong issue in recent state and national elections, on topics ranging from water policy to education practice. Similarly, educational planners are more and more aware of the self-defeating features of centralized control and are interested in finding ways to increase the flexibility of institutional executives. The clash between these philosophical views will provide grist for debate for many years to come.

Equity

We defined equity in budgeting as the provision of similar resources for similar needs, where these competing needs might be among individuals, among programs within an institution, or among institutions within a state system. To date, most efforts to measure similarity of need (particularly at the programmatic and institutional levels) have been based on fairly crude workload measures, such as the number of students by discipline and level. This operational definition of equity is certain to be challenged over the next decade. Meager advances in the understanding of the production function in education suggest to technical analysts that a one-to-one correspondence between students and resource needs is misleading. Various approaches to measuring the economy-of-scale phenomenon and incorporating it into budgetary practice are being proposed. The conditions of the next decade are likely to lead to even more fundamental equity questions. For instance, should the similarity of need be determined by counting the number of students (through an economy-of-scale technique or otherwise) or by determining the employment obligations of the institution—for example, its need not to dismiss long-term employees. This type of debate can be expected to grow especially intense at the institutional level, where budgetary flexibility is more limited and the impact of staff layoffs is most keenly felt on a personal level.

Information

Finally, information needs will continue to be a major source of contention. This will be so in part because information is relied on in most other areas of debate. But it also will be due to controversial developments in the measurement of the information itself. Perhaps the biggest hurdle to the direct application of common business budgeting practice in higher education is the lack of understanding of the production function. The cost and benefits accompanying a decision about whether to use steel or plastic in the production of some durable good are easily determined in industry. Educators, however, can seldom reach consensus concerning similar tradeoffs in the development of an educated individual. In fact, much debate continues about the goals of higher education and how they might be measured. Progress in providing this type of information for budgetary decision-making is impeded by definitional problems, but significant efforts continue. Not only are advances probable in understanding the economy of scale at institutions through measuring fixed and variable costs, there also is significant interest in the measurement of educational outcomes. Thus the provision of information will be the subject of debate at various levels for the foreseeable future—debates concerning goals, purposes, definitions, and analytical measurement techniques.

We began this monograph by citing Wildavsky's observation that "one is likely to think of budgeting as an arid subject, the province of stodgy clerks and dull statisticians." Certainly, the stodgy and the dull have their role in budgeting, along with the more vivacious and more sensitive participants. The important point, we believe, is that budget planning, through its "translation of financial resources into human purposes," should be of interest to us all. Over the next 20 years, some of the most fundamental decisions concerning the form and function of higher education are likely to be made as part of the budgeting process.

Bibliography

The ERIC Clearinghouse on Higher Education abstracts and indexes the current literature on higher education for the National Institute of Education's monthly bibliographic journal *Resources in Education (RIE)*. Most of these publications are available through the ERIC Document Reproduction Service (EDRS). Ordering number and price for publications cited in this bibliography that are available from EDRS have been included at the end of each citation. Readers who wish to order a publication should write to the ERIC Document Reproduction Service, Post Office Box 190, Arlington, Virginia 22210. When ordering, please specify the document number. Unless otherwise noted, documents are available in both microfiche (MF) and hard/photocopy (HC).

Adams, Carl R.; Hankins, Russell L.; and Schroeder, Roger G. *A Study of Cost Analysis in Higher Education*. Vol. 1: *The Literature of Cost and Cost Analysis in Higher Education*. Washington, D.C.: American Council on Education, 1978.

American Association of University Professors, Committee T on College and University Government. "The Role of the Faculty in Budgetary and Salary Matters." *AAUP Bulletin* 62 (December 1976): 379-81.

Ames, Michael Downey. "Application of Certain Business Procedures to Budgeting in Higher Education." Ph.D. dissertation, Claremont Graduate School and University Center, 1972.

Andrew, Loyd Dorsey. "From PPBS to Commitment: Case Studies of Planning Programming and Budgeting in a University Setting." Ph.D. dissertation, University of Utah, 1973.

Anthony, Robert N. *Management Accounting Principles*. Homewood, Ill.: Richard D. Irwin, 1974.

———— and Welsch, Glenn A. *Fundamentals of Management Accounting*. Homewood, Ill.: Richard D. Irwin, 1974.

Anton, Thomas J. "Agency Budget Roles." *In Public Budgeting and Finance*, edited by Robert T. Golembiewski and Jack Rubin, pp. 202-9. Itasca, Ill.: F. E. Peacock Publishers, 1975.

————, "Roles and Symbols in the Determination of State Expenditures." In *Whatever Happened to State Budgeting?*, edited by S.

Kenneth Howard and Gloria Grizzle, pp. 98-111. Lexington, Ky.: Council of State Governments, 1972.

Arnett, Trevor. *College and University Finance*. New York: General Education Board, 1922.

Astin, Alexander W., and Panos, Robert J. "The Evolution of Educational Programs." In *Educational Measurement,* edited by E. L. Thorndike, pp. 733-51. Washington, D.C.: ACE, 1971.

Bacchetti, Raymond F. "Alternative Budgeting Processes." Paper presented at the W. K. Kellogg workshops sponsored by the Centre for Administrative Studies, University of New England, Armidale, New South Wales, June-July 1978.

————. "Using Cost Analysis in Internal Management in Higher Education." *NACUBO Professional File* 9 (January 1977): 1-11. ED 136 638. MF-$0.98; HC-$2.15.

Bacon, Jeremy. *Managing the Budget Foundation*. New York: National Industrial Conference Board, 1970.

Balderston, Frederick E. *Managing Today's University*. San Francisco: Jossey-Bass, 1974.

————. "Cost Analysis in Higher Education." *California Management Review* 17 (Fall 1974): 93-107.

———— and Weathersby, George B. "PPBS in Higher Education Planning and Management: Part II, The University of California Experience." *Higher Education* 1 (August 1972): 299-319.

Baldridge, J. Victor. *Power and Conflict in the University*. New York: John Wiley and Sons, 1971.

Baldwin, Charles W. "A Decision Theory Approach to College Resource Allocation." Paper presented at the California Association for Institutional Research, 22 February 1978. ED 149 822. MF-$0.98; HC-$2.54.

Barak, Robert J. "Program Reviews by Statewide Higher Education Agencies." In *Increasing the Public Accountability of Higher Education,* edited by John K. Folger, pp. 67-90. New Directions for Institutional Research, no. 16. San Francisco: Jossey-Bass, 1977.

Benacerraf, Paul; Bowen, William G.; Davis, Thomas A.; Lewis, William W.; Morse, Linda K.; and Schafer, Carl W. *Budgeting and Resource Allocation at Princeton University*. Cited by Adams, Hankins, and Schroeder, *A Study of Cost Analysis in Higher Education*. Vol. 1: *The Literature of Cost and Cost Analysis,* p. 65. Washington, D.C.: American Council on Education, 1978.

————. *Budgeting and Resource Allocation at Princeton University*. Princeton, N.J.: Princeton University, 1972. ED 070 404. MF- $0.98; HC-$27.45.

Berdahl, Robert O. *Statewide Coordination of Higher Education.* Washington, D.C.: American Council on Education, 1971.

————, ed. *Evaluating Statewide Boards.* New Directions for Institutional Research, no. 5. San Francisco: Jossey-Bass, 1975.

————, ed. "Legislative Program Evaluation." In *Increasing the Public Accountability of Higher Education,* edited by John K. Folger, pp. 35-65. New Directions for Institutional Research, no. 16. San Francisco: Jossey-Bass, 1977.

Bogue, E. Grady, and Troutt, William E. "Allocation of State Funds on a Performance Criterion: Acting on the Possible While Awaiting Perfection." In *Research and Planning for Higher Education,* edited by Robert H. Fenske and Paul J. Staskey, pp. 45-47. Proceedings of the 17th annual forum of the Association for Institutional Research. Tallahassee, Fla.: Association for Institutional Research, 1978. ED 156 035. MF-$0.98; HC-not available.

————. *Models for Higher Education Evaluation: Explorations and Policy Intent and Impact.* Nashville: Tennessee Higher Education Commission, 1975.

Boutwell, W. K. "Formula Budgeting on the Down Side." In *Strategies for Budgeting,* edited by George Kaludis, pp. 41-50. New Directions for Institutional Research, no. 2. San Francisco: Jossey-Bass, 1973.

Bowen, Howard R. *Investment in Learning: The Individual and Social Value of American Higher Education.* San Francisco: Jossey-Bass, 1977.

Bowen, Frank M., and Glenny, Lyman A. *State Budgeting for Higher Education: State Fiscal Stringency and Public Higher Education.* Berkeley: Center for Research and Development in Higher Education, University of California, 1976. HE 010 435. MF-$0.98; HC-$15.07.

————; Ruyle, J.H.; and Glenny, L. A. *State Budgeting for Higher Education: Budget Processes in the 50 States.* Berkeley: Center for Research and Development in Higher Education, University of California, 1976.

Bower, Cathleen, and Renkiewicz, Nancy. *A Handbook for Using the Student Outcomes Questionnaires.* Boulder, Colo.: National Center for Higher Education Management Systems, 1977. ED 147 330. MF-$0.98; HC-$4.67.

Breneman, D. W. *The Ph.D. at Berkeley: Interviews, Placement, and Recommendations.* Berkeley: Ford Foundation Program for Research in University Administration, Report P-17, 1971. ED 081 376. MF-$0.98; HC-03.98.

Carnegie Commission on Higher Education. *The More Effective Use of Resources.* New York: McGraw-Hill, 1972.

Carnegie Foundation for the Advancement of Teaching. *The States and Higher Education: A Proud Past and a Vital Future.* San Francisco: Jossey-Bass, 1976.

Carter, Jimmy. "Jimmy Carter Tells Why He Will Use Zero-Base Budgeting." *Nation's Business* 65 (January 1977): 24-26.

Caruthers, Kent. "State Formula Budgeting: Issues, Perspectives, and Trends." Paper presented to the Commission on the Future of Florida's Public Universities, Tampa, Florida, 16 September 1977.

Cheit, Earl F. "The Management Systems Challenge: How to be Academic though Systematic." Paper presented at the annual meeting of the American Council on Education, Washington, D.C., 11 October 1973.

Coleman, D. R., and Bolte, J. R. "A Theoretical Approach for Internal Allocation of Academic Personnel Resources." In *Conflicting Pressures in Postsecondary Education,* edited by Robert H. Fenske, pp. 193-98. Proceedings of the 16th annual AIR forum. Tallahassee, Fla.: Air, 1977. ED 145 745. MF-$0.98; HC-$5.33.

Coleman, Jack W. "Some Practicalities of Improving Academic Management." *AACSB Bulletin* 12 (January 1975): 11-17.

Collier, Douglas J. *Higher Education Finance Manual.* Technical Report 69. Boulder, Colo.: NCHEMS at Western Interstate Commission for Higher Education [WICHE], 1975. ED 109 945. MF-$0.98; HC-$3.98.

Cope, Robert G. "Budget Formulas and Model Building." In *Institutional Research and Academic Outcomes,* pp. 163-70. Proceedings of the 8th annual AIR forum. Edited by Cameron Fincher. Athens, Ga.: Institute of Higher Education of the University of Georgia, 1968. ED 053 495. MF-$0.98; HC-$2.15.

Corbally, John E., Jr. *School Finance.* Boston: Allyn and Bacon, 1962.

Cowen, Scott S. "Zero Base Budgeting in Municipalities." Paper presented at a meeting of the Joint National ORSA/TIMS, Atlanta, Ga., November 1977.

Crecine, John P. *Governmental Problem-Solving, A Computer Simulation of Municipal Budgeting.* Chicago, Rand McNally, 1969.

Cuthbertson, Kenneth, M. "Planning and Developing the Budget." In *University Administration in Practice,* edited by Oswald Nielsen, pp. 73-88. Stanford, Calif.: Stanford University, 1959.

Cyert, Richard M., and March, James G. *A Behavioral Theory of the Firm.* Englewood Cliffs, N.J.: Prentice-Hall, 1963.

Dahl, Robert A., and Lindblom, Charles E. *Politics, Economics and Welfare*. New York: Harper, 1953.

Diesing, Paul. *Reason in Society*. Westport, Conn.: Greenwood Press, 1973.

Downs, Anthony. *Inside Bureaucracy*. Boston: Little Brown, 1967.

Dressel, Paul, and Simon, Lou Anna Kimsey. *Allocating Resources Among Departments*. New Directions for Institutional Research, no. 11. San Francisco: Jossey-Bass, 1976.

————, and Faricy, William H. *Return to Responsibility*. San Francisco: Jossey-Bass, 1972.

————; Johnson, F. Craig; and Marcus, Philip M. *The Confidence Crisis*. San Francisco: Jossey-Bass, 1970.

Dror, Yehezkel. *Public Policymaking Reexamined*. New York: Chandler Publishing, 1968.

Dunworth, John, and Cook, Rupert. "Budgetary Devolution as an Aid to University Efficiency." *Higher Education* 5 (1976): 153-67.

Federsen, William Harold. "Developing Criteria for Evaluating Budgeting in Public Community Colleges." Ed.D. dissertation, Columbia University, 1973.

Fielden, John. "The Concepts of PPBS and Approaches to Their Application." Paper presented at the Professional Seminar on Program Budgets for University Management and Planning, Paris, France, 1 October 1973.

Fincher, Cameron. "The Lust for Efficiency: A Downhome Story of the Implications of Zero-Base Budgeting." In *Research and Planning for Higher Education*, edited by Robert H. Fenske, pp. 55-57. Proceedings of the 17th annual AIR forum. Tallahassee, Fla.: Association for Institutional Research, 1976. ED 156 035. MF-$0.98; HC-not available.

Fisher, Julian F. S. "A Political Model for the University." *Educational Record* 49 (Fall 1968): 442.

Florida. Legislature. Joint Committee on Appropriations. *Report on Senate Bill 1100*. 5th Leg., 2d sess., 1978. pp. 29-30, 50-54, 58-60, 160, 165-66, 171.

Fogel, R. L. "Conditions for the Use of PPB." Cited by Adams, Hankins, and Schroeder, *A Study of the Cost Analysis in Higher Education*. Vol. 1: *The Literature of Cost and Cost Analysis*, p. 66. Washington, D.C.: American Council on Education, 1978.

Folger, John K., ed. "Editor's Notes." In *Increasing the Public Accountability of Higher Education*, pp. vii-xii. New Directions for Institutional Research, no. 16. San Francisco: Jossey-Bass, 1977.

Folger, John. "Who Wants Outcome Measures and Why Do They Want Them?" Paper presented at the Seminar on Innovation, Outcomes, and the Budget Process, San Diego, 22 March 1976.

Friedman, Milton. "Gammon's Black Holes.'" *Newsweek,* November 7, 1977, p. 84.

Furman, James M. "Budgeting: Views of a State Higher Education Director." In *Budgeting for Higher Education and the Legislative Oversight Process,* pp. 6-8. Atlanta, Ga.: Southern Regional Education Board, 1976.

Gaither, Gerald, and Johnson, Clarke C. "The Application of Zero-Base Budgeting in the University Environment." Paper presented at the 9th annual conference of the American Institute for Decision Sciences, Chicago, Ill., October 1977.

Ginsburg, Sigmund G. "Grading the Performance of University Management." *Conference Board RECORD* 12 (December 1975): 44-46.

Glenny, Lyman A. *State Budgeting for Higher Education: Interagency Conflict and Consensus.* Berkeley: Center for Research and Development in Higher Education, University of California, 1976a. ED 132 940. MF-$0.98; HC-$10.87.

———. "State Control and Programs for Higher Education." In *Budgeting for Higher Education and the Legislature Oversight Process.* Atlanta, Ga.: Southern Regional Education Board, 1976b.

———. "The Anonymous Leaders of Higher Education." *Journal of Higher Education* 43 (January 1972): 9-22.

———. *The Anonymous Leaders of Higher Education.* Berkeley: Center for Research and Development in Higher Education, University of California, 1971. ED 057 730. MF-$0.98; HC-$2.54.

———; Bowen, Frank M.; Meisinger, Richard J., Jr.; Morgan, Anthony W.; Purves, Ralph A.; and Schmidtlein, Frank A. *State Budgeting for Higher Education: Data Digest.* Berkeley: Center for Research and Development in Higher Education, University of California, 1975. ED 139 303. MF-$0.98; HC-$20.13.

Golembiewski, Robert T., and Rabin, Jack, ed. *Public Budgeting and Finance.* Itasca, Ill.: F. E. Peacock Publishers, 1975.

Graham, D. Robert. "State Budget Reform as a Way of Reforming Higher Education." Paper presented to a meeting of the Education Commission of the States, Denver, Colo., 16 December 1976.

Green, John L., Jr. *Budgeting in Higher Education.* Athens, Ga.: University of Georgia Business and Finance Office, 1971.

Greene, Calvin. "Budget Formulas Help Growing State System Tell Where It's Going." *College and University Business* 48 (June 1970): 58-64.

Gross, Francis M. "A Comparative Analysis of the Existing Budget Formulas Used for Justifying Budget Requests or Allocating Funds for the Operating Expenses of State-Supported Colleges and Universities." Monograph no. 9. Knoxville, Tenn.: University of Tennessee Office of Institutional Research, December 1973.

Gubasta, Joseph L. "Integrated Planning to Facilitate Effective Use and Reallocation of Resources." Paper presented at the annual conference of the Society for College and University Planning, Washington, D.C., July 1976. ED 126 836. MF-$0.98; HC-$2.15.

Hale, James A., and Rawson, Thomas M. "Developing Statewide Higher Education Funding Formulas for Use in a Limited Growth Environment." *Journal of Education Finance* 2 (Summer 1976): 16-32.

Halstead, D. Kent. *Statewide Planning in Higher Education*. Washington, D.C.: Government Printing Office, 1974. ED 096 914. MF-$1.98; HC-$42.30.

Hansen, W. Lee, and Weisbrod, Burton A. *Benefits, Costs, and Finance of Public Higher Education*. Chicago: Markham Publishing, 1969.

Hardy, John W. "Planning-Programming-Budgeting Systems in Universities." Cited by Adams, Hankins, and Schroeder, *A Study of Cost Analysis in Higher Education*. Vol. 1: *The Literature of Cost and Cost Analysis,* p. 66. Washington, D.C.: American Council on Education, 1978.

Harris, John. "Program Evaluation Funding: An Alternative to Funding Public Higher Education by Numbers of Students." *Southern Review of Public Administration* 1 (December 1977): 322-31.

Harvey, L. James. *Zero-Base Budgeting in Colleges and Universities*. Littleton, Colo.: Ireland Educational Corp., 1977.

Hastings, Paul G. *The Management of Business Finance*. Princeton, N.J.: D. Van Norstrand, 1966.

Hawaii State Department of Budget and Finance. *An Introduction to the State of Hawaii's Executive Budget System*. Hawaii: State Department of Budget and Finance, 1976.

Heckert, J. Brooks, and Willson, James D. *Business Budgeting and Control*. 2nd ed. New York: Ronald Press, 1955.

Heiser, Herman C. *Budgeting: Principles and Practices*. New York: Ronald Press, 1959.

Hitch, Charles J. *Decision-making for Defense*. Berkeley: University of California Press, 1967.

Hoenack, Stephen A., and Norman, Alfred L. "Incentives and Resource Allocation in Universities." *Journal of Higher Education* 45 (January 1974): 21-37.

Holmer, Freeman, and Bloomfield, Stefan D. "A Resource/Acquisition Model for a State System of Higher Education." *Planning for Higher Education* 5 (October 1976): 4/5.

Howard, S. Kenneth, and Grizzle, Gloria, eds. *Whatever Happened to State Budgeting?* Lexington, Ky.: Council of State Governments, 1972.

Howard, S. Kenneth. "Changing Concepts of State Budgeting." In *Whatever Happened to State Budgeting,* edited by S. Kenneth Howard and Gloria Grizzle, pp. 40-51. Lexington, Ky.: Council of State Governments, 1972.

————. *Changing State Budgeting.* Lexington, Ky.: Council of State Governments, 1973.

Hughes, K. Scott, and Topping, James R. "Using Cost Information and Analysis in Managing Institutional Affairs." *Business Officer* 11 (November 1977): 15-17.

Hummel, Errett, and Spalding, Willard. "How to Get Politics Out of Budget Decisions." *College and University Business* 53 (September 1972): 30-32.

Jellema, William W. "Expenditures, Deficits, and Economies." In *Strategies for Budgeting,* edited by George Kaludis, pp. 63-96. New Directions for Institutional Research, no. 2. San Francisco: Jossey-Bass, 1973.

Jones, Reginald L., and Trentin, H. George. *Budgeting: Key to Planning and Control.* New York: American Management Association, 1966.

Kaludis, George. "Emerging Principles for Budgeting." In *Strategies for Budgeting,* edited by George Kaludis, pp. 97-102. New Directions for Institutional Research, no. 2. San Francisco: Jossey-Bass, 1973.

Kellogg, Richard A. "State Controlled Higher Education in Virginia and the Budgeting Process, 1950-1972: A Move Toward Formal Methods." Ph.D. dissertation, College of William and Mary, 1974.

Kendrick, Solomon Joseph. "An Investigation of Practices and Procedures Employed in the Preparation of the Annual Budget in Selected Private Colleges and Universities in the United States." Ph.D. dissertation, American University, 1965.

Kenworthy, Walter. "A Program Budgeting Strategy for a Small College." In *Strategies for Budgeting,* edited by George Kaludis, pp. 19-40. New Directions for Higher Education, no. 2. San Francisco: Jossey-Bass, 1973.

Kerr, Clark. *The Uses of the University.* Cambridge, Mass.: Harvard University Press, 1963.

Kershaw, Joseph A., and Mood, Alex M. "Resource Allocation in Higher Education." *American Economic Review* 60 (May 1970): 341-46.

Kimbrough, Ralph B. *Political Power and Educational Decision-Making.* Chicago: Rand McNally, 1964.

Lawrence, G. Ben, and Service, Allan L., eds. *Quantitative Approaches to Higher Education Management: Potential, Limits, and Challenge.* Washington, D.C.: American Association for Higher Education, 1977. ED 144 439. MF-$0.98; HC-$6.67.

Lee, Robert D., Jr., and Johnson, Ronald W. *Public Budgeting Systems.* Baltimore, University Park Press, 1973.

LeLoup, Lance T., and Moreland, William B. "Agency Strategies and Executive Review: The Hidden Politics of Budgeting." *Public Administration Review* 38 (May/June 1978): 232-39.

Lenning, Oscar T.; Lee, Yong S.; Micek, Sidney S.; and Service, Allan L. *A Structure for the Outcomes of Postsecondary Education.* Boulder, Colo.: National Center for Higher Education Management Systems, 1977. ED 150 904. MF-$0.98; HC-$5.33.

Leslie, Larry L., and Hu, Teh-wei. *The Financial Implications of Collective Bargaining in Higher Education.* Report 29. University Park, Pa.: Center for the Study of Higher Education, 1977. ED 149 711. MF-$0.98; HC-$2.54.

————, and Johnson, Gary P. "The Market Model and Higher Education." *Journal of Higher Education* 45 (January 1974): 1-20.

Lewis, Verne B. "Toward a Theory of Budgeting." *Public Administration Review* 12 (Winter 1952): 42-54.

Lindblom, Charles E. "Incremental Decision Making." In *Public Budgeting and Finance,* edited by Robert T. Golembiewski and Jack Rabin, pp. 161-75. Itasca, Ill.: F. E. Peacock Publishers, 1975.

Lyden, Fremont James. "The Budget Cycle as a Basis for Decision Making in Higher Education." *Planning for Higher Education* 4 (October 1975): 6/6.

MacFarlane, John A. "Zero-Base Budgeting in Action." *C. A. Magazine* 109 (December 1976): 28-32.

McConnell, James LeRoy. "An Investigation of Budgeting Procedures of Selected Catholic Colleges and Universities." Ph.D. dissertation, Pennsylvania State University, 1967.

McGowan, Wayne F. "Budgeting: Perspectives from a State Executive Agency." In *Budgeting for Higher Education and the Legislative Oversight Process.* Atlanta, Ga.: Southern Regional Education Board, 1976.

McManis, Gerald L., and Harvey, L. James. *Planning, Management, and Evaluation Systems in Higher Education.* Littleton, Colo.: Ireland Educational Corp., 1978.

————, and Parker, William C. *Implementing Management Information Systems in Colleges and Universities.* Littleton, Colo.: Ireland Educational Corp., 1978.

McNamara, Robert S. *The Essence of Security: Reflections in Office.* New York: Harper and Row, 1968.

March, James G., and Simon, Herbert A. *Organizations.* New York: John Wiley and Sons, 1958.

Massy, William F. "Reflections on the Application of a Decision Science Model to Higher Education." *Decision Sciences* 9 (1978): 362-69.

Masters, Robert J., Jr., and Munsterman, Richard E. "Departmental Planning-Budgeting System (DPBS)." *Journal of Educational Data Processing* 12 (1975): 1-9.

Mathews, Fred I. "A Hard Look at Finance." *New Directions for Community Colleges* 4 (August 1976): 65-67.

Meisinger, Richard J., Jr. *State Budgeting for Higher Education: The Uses of Formulas.* Berkeley: Center for Research and Development in Higher Education, University of California, 1976. ED 132 963. MF-$0.98; HC-$16.41.

————. "The Politics of Formula Budgeting: The Determination of Tolerable Levels of Inequality through Objective Incrementalism in Public Higher Education." Ph.D. dissertation, University of California, Berkeley, 1975.

Merewitz, Leonard, and Sosnick, Stephen H. *The Budget's New Clothes.* Chicago: Rand McNally, 1971.

Micek, Sidney S. "Introducing Higher Education Outcome Information into the State Planning and Budgeting Process." Paper presented at the Seminar on Innovation, Outcomes, and the Budget Process, San Diego, 22 March 1976. ED 132 925. MF-$0.98; HC-$2.15.

————, and Jones, Dennis P. "The Federal Component of the State-Level Information Base: A Status Report of the Focused Development Work in the Educational Outcomes and Adult and Continuing Education Areas." Boulder, Colo., National Center for Higher Education Management Systems, 1978. (Typewritten.)

————; Service, Allan L.; and Lee, Yong S. *Outcome Measures and Procedures Manual.* Technical Report 70. Boulder, Colo.: National Center for Higher Education Management Systems at the Western

Interstate Commission on Higher Education, 1975. ED 115 142. MF-$0.98; HC-$6.67.

————, and Wallhaus, Robert A. *An Introduction to the Identification and Uses of Higher Education Outcome Information.* Technical Report 40. Boulder, Colo.: National Center for Higher Education Management Systems at the Western Interstate Commission on Higher Education, 1973. ED 078 781. MF-$0.98; HC-$5.33.

Michigan Department of Education. *Formula Funding Mechanisms for State Support of Public Colleges and Universities Across the Nation.* Lansing, Mich.: Michigan Department of Education, 1976. ED 131 744. MF-$0.98; HC-$3.98.

Miller, James L., Jr. "An Introduction to Budgetary Analysis." In *Introductory Papers on Institutional Research,* pp. 100-133. Atlanta, Ga.: Southern Regional Education Board, 1967.

————. *State Budgeting for Higher Education: The Use of Formulas and Cost Analysis.* Michigan Governmental Studies no. 45. Ann Arbor, Mich.: University of Michigan Institute of Public Administration, 1964.

Millett, John D. *Financing Higher Education in the United States.* New York: Columbia University Press, 1952.

Morgan, Anthony W. "Resource Allocation Reforms: Zero-Base Budgeting and Marginal Utility Analysis in Higher Education." Paper presented at a meeting of the Association for the Study of Higher Education, Chicago, Ill., 19 March 1978. ED 157 410. MF-$0.98; HC-$2.58.

————. "Flexibility for Whom: The Case of Forced Savings in Budgeting for Higher Education." *Educational Record* 56 (Winter 1975): 42-47.

Morrell, L. R. "A Look at Program Budgeting." *Educational Record* 50 (Summer 1969): 286-89.

Mortimer, Kenneth P., ed. *Faculty Bargaining, State Government and Campus Autonomy: The Experience in Eight States.* Report 87. A joint publication of the Pennsylvania State University and the Education Commission of the States. Denver, Colo.: Education Commission of the States, 1976. ED 124 224. MF-$0.98; HC-$6.67.

———— *Accountability in Higher Education.* Washington, D.C.: American Association for Higher Education, 1972.

Mosher, Frederick C. *Program Budgeting: Theory and Practice.* Chicago: Public Administration Service, 1954.

Moss, Charles E., and Gaither, Gerald H. "Formula Budgeting: Requiem or Renaissance?" *Journal of Higher Education* 47 (September/October 1976): 543-63.

Musgrave, Richard A., and Peacock, Alan T., ed. *Classics in the Theory of Public Finance.* New York: Macmillan, 1958.

Naples, Caesar J., and Caruthers, J. Kent. "The Implications for Academic Productivity of Faculty Collective Bargaining." In *Enhancing Faculty Productivity,* edited by Leonard C. Romney. Boulder, Colo.: National Center for Higher Education Management Systems, forthcoming.

National Association of College and University Business Officers. *College and University Business Administration.* 3rd ed. Washington, D.C.: National Association of College and University Business Officers, 1974.

National Committee on Standard Reports for Institutions of Higher Education. *Financial Reports for Colleges and Universities.* Chicago, Ill.: University of Chicago Press, 1935.

Navin, Leo, and Magura, Michael. "A Price Index for University Budgetary Decisions." *Journal of Higher Education* 48 (March/April 1977): 216-25.

Neff, Charles B. "Planning and Governance." *Journal of Higher Education* 42 (February 1971): 116-32.

Nelson, William C. *Program Planning Budgeting Systems for Educators.* Vol. IV: *A Research Bibliography.* Columbus, Ohio. Center for Vocational and Technical Education, 1970.

Newton, R. D. "The Application of PPBS in Higher Education: A Status Report." Paper presented at the spring conference on Program Analysis, Institute of Public Administration, Pennsylvania State University, 8 June 1972.

Odden, Allan. *School Finance Reform in the States: 1978.* Report no. F78-1. Denver, Colo.: Education Commission of the States, 1978.

Parden, Robert J. "Planning, Programming and Budgeting Systems." *Liberal Education* 57 (May 1971): 202-10.

Peterson, Marvin W. *A Synthesis of the San Diego Seminar: Innovation, Outcomes, and the State Budgeting Process.* Washington, D.C.: Postsecondary Education Convening Authority, 1976.

————. "The Potential Impact of PPBS on Colleges and Universities." *Journal of Higher Education* 42 (January 1971): 1-20.

————; Erwin, Michael; and Wilson, Richard. "State-Level Performance Budgeting." In *Increasing the Public Accountability of Higher Education,* edited by John K. Folger, pp. 1-34. New Directions for Institutional Research, no. 16. San Francisco: Jossey-Bass, 1977.

Peterson, Robert G. "Environmental and Political Determinants of State Higher Education Appropriations Policies." *Journal of Higher Education* 47 (September/October 1976): 523-42.

Pfeffer, Jeffrey, and Salancik, Gerald R. "Organizational Decision Making as a Political Process: The Case of a University Budget." *Administrative Science Quarterly* 19 (June 1974): 135-51.

Pondy, Louis R. "Towards A Theory of Internal Resource-Allocation." In *Power in Organizations,* edited by Mayer N. Zald, pp. 270-311. Nashville: Vanderbilt University Press, 1970.

Prescott, Wallace. "The Allocation and Reallocation of Financial Resources to Departments of the University." In *Reformation and Reallocation in Higher Education,* edited by Clifford T. Stewart, pp. 169-71. Proceedings of the 12th annual AIR forum. Claremont, Calif.: Claremont University Center, 1972. ED 089 557. MF-$0.98; HC-$7.54.

Purves, Ralph A., and Glenny, Lyman A. *State Budgeting for Higher Education: Information Systems and Technical Analyses.* Berkeley: Center for Research and Development in Higher Education, University of California, 1976. ED 134 114. MF-$0.98; HC-$12.71.

Pyhrr, Peter A. *Zero-Base Budgeting.* New York: John Wiley and Sons, 1973.

————. "Zero Base Budgeting." *Harvard Business Review* 49 (November/December 1970): 111-21.

Raider, Melvyn C. "A Theoretical Examination of PPBS to Determine Its Suitability as a Management Tool for a University." Paper presented at the annual meeting of the American Educational Research Association, Washington, D.C., 1975. ED 104 290. MF-$0.98; HC-$2.15.

Reeves, Floyd W. "The Cost of Education in Liberal Arts Colleges." *North Central Association Quarterly* 2 (December 1927): 248-61.

Reeves, Pascal. "Allocation of Resources Within an Institution of Higher Learning." In *Reformation and Reallocation in Higher Education,* edited by Clifford T. Stewart, pp. 167-69. Proceedings of the 12th annual AIR forum. Claremont, Calif.: Claremont University Center, 1972. ED 089 557. MF-$0.98; HC-$7.54.

Renkiewicz, Nancy, and Topping, James. *Information Exchange Procedures.* Technical Report 47. Boulder, Colo.: National Center for Higher Education Management Systems at the Western Interstate Commission on Higher Education, 1973.

Robins, Gerald B. *Understanding the College Budget.* Athens, Ga.: Institute of Higher Education, 1973.

Robinson, Daniel D.; Ray, Howard W.; and Turk, Frederick J. "Cost Behavior Analysis for Planning in Higher Education." *NACUBO Professional File* 9 (May 1977): 1-51.

Rogers, Frederick A., and Van Horn, Richard L. "Goal-Oriented Resource Allocation for University Management." In *Conflicting Pressures in Postsecondary Education,* edited by Robert H. Fenske, pp. 141-46. Proceedings of the 16th annual AIR forum. Tallahassee, Fla.: Association for Institutional Research, 1977. ED 145 745. MF-$0.98; HC-$15.07.

Rourke, Francis E., and Brooks, Glenn E. *The Managerial Revolution in Higher Education.* Baltimore: Johns Hopkins Press, 1966.

Russell, John Dale. *The Finance of Higher Education Revised Edition.* Chicago: University of Chicago Press, 1954.

Ruyle, J. H., and Glenny, L. A. *State Budgeting for Higher Education: Trends in State Revenue Appropriations from 1968-75.* Berkeley: Center for Research and Development in Higher Education, University of California, 1976.

Sarant, Peter C. *Zero-Base Budgeting in the Public Sector.* Reading, Mass.: Addison-Wesley Publishing, 1978.

Schick, Allen. *Budget Innovation in the States.* Washington, D.C.: Brookings Institution, 1971.

———. "The Road to PPB: The Stages of Budget Reform." *Public Administration Review* 26 (December 1966): 243-58.

Schmidtlein, Frank A., and Glenny, Lyman A. *State Budgeting for Higher Education: The Political Economy of the Process.* Berkeley: Center for Research and Development in Higher Education, University of California, 1977. ED 138 171. MF-$0.98; HC-$16.41.

Schultze, Charles L. *The Politics and Economics of Public Spending.* Washington, D.C.: Brookings Institution, 1968.

Simpson, William B. "Constraining Ratio Approach to Allocating Instructional Resources." *Socio-Economic Sciences* 9 (1975): 285-92.

Smith, Lester S. "The Allocation of Financial Resources in Higher Education." Paper presented for Education 925.35, a course at Ohio State University, Autumn quarter 1967.

SMU Institute of Technology. *1973 Annual Report.* Dallas, Tex.: Southern Methodist University, 1973.

Spence, David S. *Formula Funding in the SREB States.* Atlanta, Ga.: Southern Regional Education Board, 1978.

Stedry, Andrew C. "Budgets: Definition and Scope." In *Public Budgeting and Finance,* pp. 6-14. Edited by Robert T. Golembiewski and Jack Rabin. Itasca, Ill.: F. E. Peacock Publishers, 1975.

Stonich, Paul J. *Zero-Base Planning and Budgeting.* Homewood, Ill.: Dow Jones-Irwin, 1977.

Strom, James L. "Do Budget Appropriation Formulae Produce Accurate Teaching Support Dollars?" *Planning for Higher Education* 6 (October 1977): 21-26.

Stuart, Douglas A. "The Application of Formula and Cost Analysis Procedures to the Budgeting of Academic Departments." Ph.D. dissertation, Michigan State University, 1966.

Stumph, Wayne Julius. "A Comparative Study of Statewide Operating Budget Formulas Administered by Statewide Coordinating Agencies for Higher Education in Selected States." Ph.D. dissertation, Southern Illinois University, 1970.

Subcommittee of Intergovernmental Relations. *Compendium of Materials on Zero-Base Budgeting in the States.* Washington, D.C.: Government Printing Office, 1977.

Summers, F. William. "The Use of Formulae in Resource Allocation." *Library Trends* 23 (April 1975): 631-42.

Thompson, Donald L. "PPBS: The Need for Experience." *Journal of Higher Education* 42 (November 1971): 678-91.

Thompson, James D. *Organizations in Action.* New York: McGraw-Hill, 1967.

Tickton, Sidney G. "Meeting the Financial Pinch." *Compact* 5 (October 1971): 30-33.

Toler, Thomas M. *PPBS: Its Impact Upon Curriculum Decisions.* Arlington, Va.: ERIC Document Reproduction Service, 1977. ED 136 897. MF-$0.98; HC-$19.27.

Topping, James. *Cost Analysis Manual.* Technical Report 45. Boulder, Colo.: National Center for Higher Education Management Systems at the Western Interstate Commission on Higher Education, 1974. ED 093 249. MF-$0.98; HC-$19.27.

Tucker, John M. "Coping with the Squeeze of the New Seller's Market." *Business Officer* 12 (April 1978): 16-18.

Turrisi, Ilona. "Obtaining Departmental Resources through Planning, Analysis, and Persuasion." Draft of a working paper to be included in workshop manual for Institute for Departmental Leadership, Tallahassee, Fla., Florida State University, 1978.

U.S. General Accounting Office. *Planning-Programming-Budgeting and Systems Analysis Glossary.* Washington, D.C.: Government Printing Office, 1968.

Van Wijk, Alfons P., and Levine, Jack B. "The Pros and Cons of Existing Formula Financing Systems and a Suggested New Approach." Paper presented at the Colleges of Applied Arts and Technology Design Workshop, Ottawa, Canada, 18 November 1969. ED 132 994. MF-$0.98; HC-$8.01.

Wattenbarger, James L., and Starnes, Paul M. *Financial Support Patterns for Community Colleges, 1976.* Gainsville, Fla.: Institute of Higher Education of Florida University, 1976.

Weathersby, George B., and Jackson, Gregory A. "Individual Demand for Higher Education: A Review and Analysis of Recent Empirical Studies." Paper presented at NACUBO 1975 Assessment of Financial Health of Small Colleges Workshop, Washington, D.C., 8-10 October 1975.

Weinberg, William M. "Patterns of State-Institutional Relations Under Collective Bargaining." In *Faculty Bargaining, State Government and Campus Autonomy: The Experience in Eight States,* edited by Kenneth P. Mortimer, pp. 95-106. Published jointly by Pennsylvania State University and Education Commission of the States. Report 87. Denver, Colo.: Education Commission of the States, 1976. ED 124 224. MF-$0.98; HC-$6.67.

Wildavsky, Aaron. *Budgeting, A Comparative Theory of Budgetary Processes.* Boston: Little Brown, 1975.

————. *The Politics of the Budgetary Process.* 2nd ed. Boston: Little Brown, 1974.

Wiles, David K. "Policy Adaptation in Higher Education: Fundamental Issues of Allocation and Legitimacy." *Journal of Education Finance* 2 (Winter 1977): 286-304.

Williams, Harry. *Planning for Effective Resource Allocation in Universities.* Washington, D.C.: American Council on Education, 1966.

Williams, Jack K. "Budgeting: A University Perspective." In *Budgeting for Higher Education and the Legislative Oversight Process,* pp. 1-5. Atlanta, Ga.: Southern Regional Education Board, 1976.

Wishart, Patricia, and Rossman, Jack. *Career Patterns, Employment, and Earnings of Graduates of Eleven ACM Colleges.* Final report to the Fund for the Improvement of Postsecondary Education, Grant no. G007503559. Chicago: Associated Colleges of the Midwest, 1977.

Ziemer, Gordon; Young, Michael; and Topping, James. *Cost Finding Principles and Procedures.* Technical Report 26. Boulder, Colo.: National Center for Higher Education Management Systems at the Western Interstate Commission on Higher Education, 1971. ED 074 883. MF-$0.98; HC-$17.93.

Already Published in the 1979 Series

1. Women in Academe: Steps to Greater Equality — $4.00
   Judith Gappa and Barbara Uehling

2. Old Expectations, New Realities: The
   Academic Profession Revisited — $4.00
   Carol Herrnstadt Shulman

To subscribe to the Research Report series (10 issues starting from date of subscription), write to the Publications Department, American Association for Higher Education, One Dupont Circle, Suite 780, Washington, D.C. 20036.